STORIES OF
Ganesha

SHUBHA VILAS

PRAKASH

Reprint 2023

PRAKASH

An imprint of Prakash Books India Pvt. Ltd.

113/A, Darya Ganj,
New Delhi-110 002
Email: info@prakashbooks.com/sales@prakashbooks.com

facebook www.facebook.com/fingerprintpublishing
twitter www.twitter.com/FingerprintP
www.fingerprintpublishing.com

ISBN: 978 93 5440 086 5

Processed & printed in India

INTRODUCTION TO GANESHA

Ganesha is arguably one of the most loved and revered personalities in the Vedic pantheon. He has many names that point out to his different aspects. The word Ganesha comes from the two root words, *Gana* and *isha.* Gana means people and isha means the Lord. Thus, Ganesha literally means Lord of the people. But the word Gana refers to both the common man as well as the Ganas or the hobgoblin disciples of Lord Shiva. Ganapati also refers to the same thing, the master of the Ganas.

He is also called *Vighna Vinashaka* or *Vighnaharta.* Vighna means obstacles. Vinashaka means destroyer and Harta means the one who steals away. Thus,

Vighna Vinashaka means the one who destroys obstacles on one's path and Vighnaharta means the one who steals away all obstacles on one's path. For Vaishnavas, Lord Ganesha removes the obstacles on their path of devotion to Lord Vishnu. For most people, this simply means that he removes all obstacles that prevent a person from experiencing peace, prosperity, and joy.

Perhaps the most unique distinguishing and simultaneously intriguing aspect of Lord Ganesha for anyone disconnected from the Vedic fold is his elephant-head that gives him the name Gajanana, which simply means elephant-headed. Usually an elephant has two tusks but Ganesha stands out with a singular tusk and is thus called Ekadanta, which means the one with a single tusk. You will find details of all these stories within the pages of this book and many more secrets of Lord Ganesha that you probably didn't know of.

Considered the god of prosperity, he literally looks prosperous. The words Lambodara (which means the one who has a potbelly or hanging belly) and Mahodara (which means the one who has a great belly) are indicative of his prosperous size.

To top it all, Ganesha always carries sweets in his hands which make him look visually delightful. There is a unique snake belt that holds his belly together, giving him a mystic look, like his father Lord Shiva.

What makes this package the most amazing one is that he rides on a tiny mouse. Imagine a huge personality fitting perfectly on the back of a tiny mouse. This is the combination of prosperity riding on simplicity.

One of Ganesha's most beautiful names is Buddhipriya, which means the one who loves intelligence or the one who is the husband of intelligence. He is considered the god of learning and wisdom.

I remember as a child when I had to attend an exam or begin any work that required intelligence, my parents would often tell me to write Shri Ganesha in tiny letters on the upper corner of the paper. This was to invoke the infinite wisdom of Ganesha in one's endeavours. Due to his contribution to the writing of *Mahabharata*, acting as a scribe of Veda Vyasa, Ganesha's connection with the literary world is deep. He is considered to be the god of letters.

Ganesha's family itself is unique and so are the animals associated with them. Lord Shiva is his father and a snake adorns his body in place of ornaments. Goddess Parvati is his mother and she rides a tiger. Kartikeya is his brother and he rides a peacock.

The interesting observation is that the mouse is the food of the snake, the snake is food of the peacock and the peacock is eaten by the tiger. Though these four animals are natural enemies, when they are connected to this family, all enmity is forgotten and they serve together lovingly. Differences in personalities is not a basis for the absence of love and cooperation. When there is respect, love and cooperation are natural.

Ganesha is married to Riddhi (prosperity), Siddhi (spiritual power), and Buddhi (intelligence) and he has two sons Shubha (auspiciousness) and Labha (profit). This book, a beautiful meditation on this most special personality, is a collection of handpicked stories from various scriptures. It will enlighten you about Lord Ganesha and help you see the many beautiful facets of his divine personality.

Most of the stories from this book mention sources, but in some stories, where the source is unknown it is clearly indicated. In no way is this book a work of scholarship but rather, a book for meditation and absorption—to pay one's respects to one of the most revered personalities in the Vedic texts.

I invite readers to delve into these delectable stories and derive great inspiration and connection with Lord Ganesha, who will help us attain our desired goals.

Here are some special prayers to offer to Lord Ganesha and connect with his blessings.

Vakratunda Maha-Kaaya Surya-Kotti Samaprabha
Nirvighnam Kuru Me Deva Sarva-Kaaryeshu Sarvadaa

Translation: Oh god with a curved trunk and a large body; your aura is like the effulgence of millions of suns. Please remove all obstacles forever that come in the way of my actions.

Aum Ekadantaya Viddhamahe, Vakratundaya Dhimahi,
Tanno Danti Prachodayat

Translation: We pray to the omnipresent one with a single-tusk. We meditate upon the one with curved elephant shaped trunk praying for greater intellect. We bow before the one with the single-tusked elephant tooth to illuminate our minds with wisdom.

yat-pada-pallava-yugam vinidhaya kumbha-
dvandve pranama-samayesa ganadhirajaha
vighnan vihantum alam asya jagat-trayasya
govindam adi-purusham tam aham bhajami

Translation: I adore the primordial Lord Govinda, whose lotus feet are always held by Ganesha on the mounds protruding from his elephant head in order to attain power for his role in destroying all obstacles that hamper progress of the three worlds.

Spoken by Brahma to Lord Govinda, in Brahma Samhita (Chapter 5 Verses 1, 29 – 56) composed by Vyasadeva.

I pray that this book helps readers not only to enhance their connection with Lord Ganesha but also helps remove all obstacles on their path of devotion and life's fulfilment.

Shubha Vilas

CONTENTS

SECTION 2:

SECTION 1:

Stories of Ganesha

1.
THE STORY OF MAHOTKATA

Aditi was the proud mother of the *devatas*. It was a fulfilling experience for her, no doubt. Why then, did she feel incomplete? For some days now, she had been experiencing a deep-seated longing. A sense of dissatisfaction had enveloped her being. She, in fact, yearned to be the mother of a divine child.

When she discussed this with her husband, Sage Kashyapa, he encouraged her to meditate on Ganesha. Since it was Satya *yuga*, meditation was the primary mode of dharma. Following his sensible advice, Aditi began her *tapasya*, which continued for a hundred years.

Seeing that she was not willing to slow down even after a century, Lord Ganesha finally appeared before her. At first, Ganesha's sudden appearance with ten hands and a snake tied around his belly frightened Aditi. Ganesha was at his sparkling best, dressed in fine jewellery and garlands. Calming Aditi's nerves, he declared how pleased he was with her devotion. Aditi then opened her heart to him, asking for a son just like him. A son who would never tire of destroying demons and saving the good-hearted. Ganesha assured Aditi that he himself, the elephant-headed God, would appear in her womb and take up the mantle of subduing demonic onslaughts in the world.

Elsewhere, two brahman brothers, Narantaka and Devantaka were following exactly the same process of austerities to please Lord Shiva. Lord Shiva, who is known as Ashutosha or one who is easily pleased, bestowed on them the boon they desired: to be unstoppable in their conquests. Once they achieved their wish, they went on a rampage. Narantaka captured the earth and the lower planets while Devantaka went higher up to conquer the heavenly planets.

Between the two of them, they ruled everything under the sky. With time, their atrocities grew as there was no one who could challenge their power. The fact that that the two brothers would only become progressively unbearable, was not lost on the devatas. When they prayed for someone to save them, there was a celestial announcement. Their saviour Ganesha would take birth as the son of Kashyapa muni and Aditi to put an end to their miseries.

The divine child that came was called Mahotkata—the elephant-headed Vinayaka with a single tusk and ten arms. The demonic brothers got wind of the news that a child was born with the single-minded purpose of eliminating them. They sent Viraja, a female demon, to destroy the new arrival. But she was no match for the powerful Mahotkata. The news of her death rattled the brothers. Viraja was very powerful and her death meant their enemy was even more powerful. This was a cause for concern. They immediately sent two more demons to kill Mahotkata. The demons went as parrots. The parrots found Aditi feeding the child. It was a good time to attack, taking the child by surprise. But the minute they approached, Vinayaka caught the birds with surprising agility and strangled their necks with so much ease that it seemed as if they were stuffed birds. The parrots choked and immediately revealed their original forms, shocking everyone. Kashyapa then realised that he was blessed with a divine son.

When Mahotkata was five years old, it was time for the *yagyopavita* ceremony. Many brahmans were invited to bless the child. Taking advantage of the situation, many demons also entered, disguised as brahmans. They thought that no one would guess that demons were present, and they could kill the enemy very easily, unhindered. They sneaked in their weapons hidden inside their *kamandalus* and attacked Vinayaka in the middle of the ceremony. Vinayaka reflexively threw some rice grains at them and the demons were instantly killed. The ceremony then went on peacefully and the brahmans blessed Vinayaka heartily.

Soon Vinayaka was old enough to assist his father Kashyapa in conducting *yagyas.* The king of Kashi once came to ask Kashyapa muni to perform the marriage ceremony of his son. Since he was busy, he asked his son Vinayaka to accompany the king back to Kashi and conduct the marriage. The journey was long and they were crossing a forest.

Unknown to them, a demon was waiting there as well. He had acquired a powerful glittering weapon by meditating on Lord Surya, who had happily gifted him a weapon that could conquer all *lokas*. As the demon waited gleefully to bask in the success of killing Mahotkata, the latter had other plans for him. One moment he was gloating with the special weapon in his hand and the next moment, the weapon was no longer in his hand. In a flash, Mahotkata had snatched the weapon away. And killed him with the same weapon. The king could not help being impressed with the rare courage he had just witnessed.

The demon who had been killed happened to be the uncle of Narantaka and Devantaka. They were mad with rage on hearing the tragic news. The demon's sons too saw red and without thinking rushed to take revenge. After a bloody battle with them, Vinayaka killed them too. But some people don't learn any lessons from experience, do they? The demon's wife now wanted revenge. An eye for an eye. She had lost her husband and two sons. In return she wanted to kill their killer. Thinking of a wicked plan, she offered Vinayaka a bottle of oil. It was an inflammable oil and the minute Vinayaka opened the bottle, it burst into flames. Flames from a small bottle of oil to burn the divine Ganesha? That's how foolish demons can be. Vinayaka threw a coconut on her head and the demoness never breathed again.

On reaching Kashi, he finally killed Narantaka and Devantaka and fulfilled the purpose of his birth.

Ganesha appears on different vehicles in different yugas. While in Satya yuga, hc is born to Sage Kashyapa and Aditi and mounts a lion, in Treta yuga he is on the peacock with Shiva and Parvati as his parents.

Source – Ganesha Purana

2.
THE STORY OF GAJANAN – HOW GANESHA GOT HIS ELEPHANT HEAD

Mothers feel the happiest when they see their children. As a mother, Parvati was no exception. Her joy knew no bounds when her son Kartikeya played in her lap. His innocent chatter and laughter brought sunshine into her life. But she secretly longed for another child. The more the better. But would her ascetic husband, Lord Shiva agree? He was always absorbed in meditation, far away from thoughts of expanding his family. But expand she had to. She would figure out a way.

At the first moment of privacy she got with her husband, she bared her heart to him. Her body was tensed and mind worried, anticipating the worst. But she immediately relaxed when Shiva agreed to her suggestion. In fact, he suggested that she take a vow to please Lord Vishnu with *kirtan*, offerings of flowers, lamps, garlands, and other items of worship. It was the same vow that Suniti, wife of Utpanpada, had taken to obtain Dhruva. And Kuber's wife to obtain Nalakuvera. Brihaspati, guru of devatas, was also a result of this vow as was Shukracharya, the guru of demons. Parvati willingly agreed to implement this elevating proposal from Mahadeva. She listened carefully to the instructions for the entire process from Lord Shiva and then proceeded to fulfil the vow by meditating on Lord Vishnu.

A few days into her meditation, she was suddenly shaken out of her reverie by a bright ball of light. The light was blinding—as if thousands of suns were glaring at her. From the fiery element, stepped out the object of her meditation. Lord Vishnu . . . looking absolutely divine, with a smile that conquers His devotees and draped in sunflower yellow with His trademark weapons in His hands. His presence thrilled Parvati. Looking at Him, only one thought occupied her mind. 'How I wish I had a son like dear Lord Vishnu!' It was the single-most thought in her mind that occupied her entire being. Sensing her desire, Lord Vishnu said, "Your wish will be fulfilled." And He disappeared in a flash, leaving behind a dazed Parvati.

Having completed her vow, a happy Parvati distributed gifts to brahmanas. At the end of the day, she finally had some quiet time with Lord Shiva. While they were in private ecstasy, a knock shattered the silence of the night. Alarmed, they asked who it was. The voice from outside their door asked for some food. It was a hungry mendicant who had heard that she was giving away gifts in charity.

Always eager to serve one and all, Parvati welcomed the guest although he had arrived at an odd hour. She went inside to fetch him some gifts but when she returned, he was nowhere in sight. Strange! Where could he have gone? she wondered. She looked here and there hoping to spot him. She peeped outside the door. Had he left? Had she offended him in some way?

Unable to comprehend the mendicant's behaviour, she was about to follow him out when she heard a divine announcement. It was a voice from above that said, "Go inside, not outside. You have been blessed with a newborn child who is on your bed. The mendicant who came was Lord Vishnu himself."

She rushed in to see if that was true. And what did she see? Lying on her bed was the most adorable baby in the whole world kicking his legs in the air. He was making baby sounds that sounded like a well-orchestrated symphony to Parvati's ears. She rushed to him and hugged him, pulling him into her embrace. In a matter of a few moments, her world had changed.

Lord Shiva was overjoyed too and together they hugged and kissed the child. The next day, Shiva announced the arrival of the newborn and gave away unprecedented amounts of charity. Gifts flowed like a monsoon river . . . joyous and abundant. Everyone queued up to have a look at the wonder baby, a gift of Vishnu himself. Devatas, gandharvas, kinnaras . . . all were eager to shower their blessings on Parvati's bundle of joy. Everyone was impatient to reach the cradle. Amongst them was also Shani, son of the Sun God. He took permission from Brahma, Shiva, and others to visit the newborn.

When he entered the chamber, he bent his head low. Keeping his eyes half closed as in meditation, he approached the cot. But when he did not open his eyes or bend his head towards the baby to see him, Parvati got suspicious. 'Why are you not looking at the baby?' she demanded from him. How dare he come till here and not even glance at her baby. Shani had put Parvati off.

"Oh goddess, please hear me out. Once when I was in meditation, my wife expressed her desire to be with me. But because I was so absorbed in worship, I did not hear her, nor look at her. In anger, she cursed me. Whoever I look at, will get destroyed. So now I don't glance at anyone at all, lest something bad happens. Please forgive me. But it is for your own good." A devastated Shanideva revealed his dilemma.

But Parvati would not hear of this. "You have come thus far. So please see my son and bless him." She insisted. Knowing well that he could not argue with Parvati, Shani turned his face to see the baby, that too from the corner of one eye.

As soon as his glance fell upon the child, the baby's head separated from his body and flew out of the window, out of the house, zooming across the sky.

The scene of her baby without his head paralysed Parvati. She fell unconscious on the floor. Shiva too was dumbstruck. How could this be happening to him?

To normalise the situation, Vishnu went to River Pushpabhadra where He found a bull elephant on the riverbank. The elephant was a gandharva, cursed to become an animal and waiting for his liberation. Vishnu shot his disc, the Sudarshan Chakra, which went and cut the elephant's head. Taking the head with Him, Vishnu returned to Shiva's abode and placed the head on the baby. Once again, the child came alive, squealing and kicking his legs. Seeing him hale and hearty, the festivities continued.

Since the child now had an elephant's head, he came to be known as Gajanan.

Source – Brahma-vaivarta Purana

3.

THE STORY OF GANANAYAK – THE DANCING GANESHA

For the world, Ganesha is the one who removes all obstacles, and harbingers success. But for his parents and loved ones, he was a fountainhead of mischief. Ganesha loved to get all the attention he could demand from them. Not that Shiva and Parvati minded. They found him too cute and adorable, and recorded all his hilarious actions which they could narrate to him later. Parvati loved telling every visitor who came to Kailash about how smart her son was.

One day Brahma happened to meet Parvati. And Parvati was more than happy to describe Ganesha's antics. They were enjoying a pleasant discussion together when Brahma remembered a scene. He was eager to share what he had seen with Mother Parvati.

At the time of universal destruction, he had seen a banyan leaf floating in the vast expanse of water. Startled, he rubbed his eyes and looked again to check whether his eyes were deceiving him. What was a banyan leaf doing in the middle of this ocean when everything had been destroyed? He inched closer to take a peek at what was floating on the leaf. The minute he peeped at the leaf, he was in for a surprise. Splash! A spray of icy cold water hit his face.

For a moment, he didn't know what got him. He quickly wiped the water off his face, ready to yell at the person who had played this prank. But all his anger evaporated when he saw an innocent smiling face looking up at him. It was a round cuddly baby with an elephant head, smiling sweetly. The baby had collected water in his trunk and sprayed it on him. Brahma burst out laughing at the naughty child who stared at him with his eyes twinkling. The baby reciprocated his laughter and cooed delightfully. Brahma's anger had turned into merriment, and he laughed like never before.

He admitted to Parvati that it was the sweetest moment of his life; the time he set his eyes on little Ganesha and his adorable sense of humour. Parvati cackled gleefully, marvelling at how easily her baby Ganesha captured hearts. His very persona lent warmth and positivity to all those who came in contact with him.

She remembered a time when she was breastfeeding her younger son Kartikeya. Ganesha was a little older, so she thought Kartikeya needed her milk more than him. But Ganesha did not agree with this, as she soon realised. The minute he saw Kartikeya getting his mother's love and not him, he stomped towards his mother. In his haste, he even lost his balance, stumbled, and nearly fell.

Somehow, he reached Parvati and latched onto her to suckle her. He suckled with such fervour as if to get as much milk out of her as he could before his competitor Kartikeya could outdo him. He suckled as if he had been starving for days. Only when he was sure that he had achieved his goal did he stop suckling to give his dear mother a contented smile. Parvati hugged him assuring him of her love for him.

Lord Shiva was watching the entire saga with amusement and pronounced Ganesha to be a glutton. Ganesha didn't care and he hugged his mother back, squeezing her tightly, unwilling to let her go. His warm touch still lingered on her skin, as if it was just a few seconds ago.

Kartikeya was no less. He was well aware that Ganesha often encroached upon his rights and territory. But being younger, he had to plan strategically to get his quota of love from his mother.

One day, he saw Mother Parvati kissing Ganesha on his head. Ganesha being Ganesha, wanted this to go on and remained stationary, refusing to move. Kartikeya could not bear it any longer and he too came running. Quietly he climbed into his mother's lap drawing her attention to him.

When Parvati noticed Kartikeya's presence in her lap, she shifted her attention to him. Kissing and stroking him in the same way, she ruffled his hair and showered her love on him. That's how Kartikeya managed to get more kisses from his mother.

Like his father, Ganesha too loved to dance. He had grace and poise, and a sense of rhythm; qualities that made him a versatile dancer. Often, Lord Shiva would ask Ganesha to dance for him. Shiva was Nataraja, and he felt immense pride in watching Ganesha move his feet.

Once it so happened that many demigods had come to Kailash to visit Shiva. Everyone was in a light mood and Shiva asked Ganesha to perform for all the demigods. Ganesha obliged, at the request of his father. His hands and feet glided in the air, following the beat of the drums. His movements flowed with such ecstatic grace that it took away the breath of the audience. An elated Shiva then gave Ganesha the title of 'Gananayak'—a hero amongst all.

Source – Folk Tales

4.
PANCHAJANYA AND VALAMPURI GANESHA

Vishnu woke up startled, His yoga *nidra* disturbed. Something was drastically wrong. He felt an acute loss in His heart. Something dear to Him had been taken away. Who was foolish enough to rob Him? It was preposterous even to imagine that. But unbelievably, someone had broken in while He was sleeping and taken away something from Him.

Instinctively, He looked for His conch shell. His Panchajanya. Panchajanya was always with Him. When He blew on His conch shell, His enemies would begin their final countdown. He had retrieved it from the depths of Prabhasa ocean after killing a demon who lived inside this conch shell. Something about the conch shell had attracted Him to it—as if it was something that had always belonged to Him. And after finishing the demon off, He had happily tucked the magnetic object inside His dhoti. Since then, Panchajanya had been an extension of His persona. His companion at all times. He always blew it to signal the victory of good over evil.

What He loved about Panchajanya was They made a great team together. The divine sound from the conch shell reverberated across the world just the way He wanted. Hearing this sound, the demonic felt acute fear and the saintly felt reassured that help was coming.

Suddenly jolted out of His reverie at the sound of a conch shell blowing, Vishnu looked around for His Panchajanya. It was missing. He had instinctively known that someone had taken away His Panchajanya and that had broken His sleep. And not only was it missing but someone was blowing on it too. Vishnu marvelled at the audacity of the thief. Surely, there was some mystery behind this. An ordinary person wouldn't dare to do this.

The *shankhanaad* or the sound of his conch shell was still ringing in His ears. It was the distinct sound of His very own Panchajanya, a sound so close to His heart He could recognise it even if unconscious. What alarmed Him further was the direction from which the vibration was coming. He recoiled in horror at the very realisation. It was being blown from Mount Kailash.

That could only mean one thing. Shiva was behind this atrocity. Nothing could happen on Kailash Mountain without his implicit approval. He also knew Shiva's penchant for conch shells. In fact, his name Shankara possibly originated from there. Shankha – kara – meaning blower of the conch. It all made sense. Without wasting a moment, Vishnu headed towards Shiva's snowy abode.

As Vishnu got closer to Mount Kailash, the sound of Panchajanya grew louder. Someone was continually blowing enthusiastically on His conch shell. He allowed Himself a fleeting smile at the feverish fervour of the culprit. A scowl quickly replaced the smile because it was His Panchajanya after all. Entering Shiva's abode with long strides, He quickly located Shiva. Shiva smiled indulgently as he gazed towards his son Ganesha, his fatherly pride written all over his face.

"Return my Panchajanya immediately!"

Shiva turned to Vishnu. He had not expected Vishnu to come so soon. No doubt he had borrowed His conch shell, but it was only for Ganesha. Ganesha wanted to experience blowing the one and only Panchajanya. Panchajanya was a *Valampuri Shankh*, which means it is a right-handed conch, said to be very auspicious. Blowing on it heralded wealth and intelligence. So, Shiva had fulfilled Ganesha's desire. No harm in it, was there? But judging by Vishnu's expression, it was a serious matter.

"It's with Ganesha. See how much he loves it?" Lord Shiva replied sheepishly, trying to pacify Lord Vishnu.

"Okay, please ask Ganesha to give it back to Me." That was a simple enough request, Lord Vishnu thought.

"I can, but he won't. I know him well. He won't return it till we pamper him and make him feel important all day. Only then will he decide to part with it."

Vishnu stared at Shiva, expecting him to find a way out. How to get back the conch shell was Shiva's problem, not His.

Getting no reply from Vishnu, Shiva tried to clarify, "If you spend one day here and pamper Ganesha, make him feel important, then he will happily give it back."

Both Lord Shiva and Lord Vishnu knew it was an absurd request. But Vishnu wanted His conch shell back and Shiva wanted his son happy. So, Vishnu gave in and agreed to the plea.

He spent the day with little Ganesha who was happily holding the conch in his trunk turned to the right in order to blow the Valampuri conch. Since then, Ganesha with his trunk on the right side is known as Valampuri Ganesha.

Ganesha is not seen often with his trunk on the right side. His more popular posture is with his trunk on the left side. This is known as Vamamukhi Ganesha. The left-side-trunk Ganesha stands for prosperity and wealth. Left also represents the moon which brings in peace and bliss. And significantly, Parvati is seated to the left of Shiva, so Ganesha is paying obeisance to his mother too and ushering in harmony and happiness at home and in relationships.

The right side stands for freedom from material desires and liberation. Temples, therefore, are places where we see the right-side-trunk Ganesha. Householders cannot give up worldly pleasures. Just as the left side represents moon, the right side represents sun. The sun stands for creation as well as destruction. The right-side-trunk Valampuri Ganesha is symbolic of the energy of the sun or *Pingala nadi* and if not cared for can even destroy happiness. He is worshipped with Vedic rituals and customs.

And to complete the story, Lord Vishnu did what Lord Shiva wanted Him to do and ultimately, Ganesha, overjoyed at all the attention he was getting from the Supreme Lord Vishnu, offered the Panchajanya conch to Lord Vishnu. The Panchajanya was relieved to return to its rightful owner too.

Source – Ganesha Purana

5.
A LIFE-LESSON FOR GANESHA FROM HIS MOTHER

It was always a tough task to keep his eyes open after a heavy meal, and tougher still to balance his huge potbelly over his legs in a comfortable position and snooze. But when the goddess of sleep made her way, no discomforts could stop her. Little Ganesha drifted into a warm and fuzzy sleep dreaming of *modaks* waiting for him on waking. Barely had he closed his eyes when he was jolted back to consciousness by some scurrying activity around him.

Reluctant to open both his eyes, he peered from one eye to ascertain the cause of commotion. Was it a demon or were it devatas? It was always either of the two. Demons came for boons and devatas came for help. But to come and disturb his sleep was a bit more than what little Ganesha wanted to tolerate. He had not even begun dreaming of modaks!

From the corner of his half open eye, he saw neither demons nor devatas. Jumping frantically at his feet and running here and there was his mouse Krauncha. Now why was he behaving like a dancing buffoon? He closed his eye again, eager to catch his forty winks. But Krauncha had other ideas.

"Ganesha, it's me, wake up, wake up!"

Ganesha heard but he did not respond. Krauncha looked around for a safe hiding place but there was none. His only hope to survive was getting Ganesha into action.

"A cat is going to gobble me up soon. I'm afraid of this monstrous cat Ganesha."

He tried to yell but half the words died in his throat as Krauncha trembled like a leaf in a storm.

"Cat?"

Now Ganesha opened both his eyes. The cat had piqued his curiosity. He hardly ever saw any animal at his abode, Mount Kailash. No wonder

Krauncha was in a tizzy. Mouse and cat had been sworn enemies since the time of creation.

Having got Ganesha out of his slumber, Krauncha stood on his hind feet and with folded hands explained the situation.

"Please forgive me for disturbing your sleep but it is a question of my life. I have been attacked by a cat and it's an emergency situation."

Krauncha continued to give a full report on how the cat had sneaked in and was waiting to pounce on him.

"Krauncha, what is there to worry?" Ganesha was now not only fully awake, but his head was teeming with naughty pranks to indulge in at the expense of the cat. With a sparkle in his eyes, he went giddy thinking of the excitement waiting ahead.

He laughed merrily and said, "Krauncha, call all your friends."

Soon a nest of mice huddled around Ganesha. Krauncha's friends and siblings. They listened attentively as Ganesha spelled out his wicked plan. Then they advanced gleefully towards the cat with Ganesha mounted on Krauncha leading the way.

The poor cat had palpitations when she saw the army of mice headed by an elephant-faced boy coming her way. One single cat could not possibly fight an army of mice. Afraid for herself, she took a few steps back, trying to keep a safe distance between them. The mice bullies quickly formed a circle around her sealing her escape routes. They went menacingly around in circles. Then they chased her from one side to another, enjoying her distress.

When the mice had had their fun, Ganesha stepped in. He picked up the cat by her tail and swung her like a pendulum. The cat oscillated upside down, side to side. Next, he twirled her in the air going round and round himself. The cat shrieked in pain as the mice jumped up and down clapping in glee, thoroughly enjoying the show put up by Ganesha. Finally, Ganesha let go off the cat's tail leaving it to crash on the ground. Even after that, he chased her till she finally collapsed into a heap.

Ganesha remembered that it was time to gobble sweet modaks. Leaving the scene, he ran off to find his mother Parvati. He told the mice to wait so that he could arrange food for all of them. His mother was always waiting for him with freshly baked modaks at the exact time he got hungry. But today, he couldn't see her. He peeped into her room and saw her on her bed, moaning in pain. Alarmed to see her bruised and blue, covered with dust, he ran towards her.

"Mother, mother, what happened to you? Who hurt you?"

A tear rolled down his cheek to see his mother's pain.

Parvati hugged him tight and smiled broadly.

"Don't you remember you and your nest of mice were playing with me thinking I'm a cat?"

Ganesha was shell-shocked. Was she saying that he hurt her? His mind went numb as a wave of panic surged through his body.

"I am the mother of the entire existence. Every living entity is part of me. When you hurt a part of this creation, you hurt me as well. So, it's because of your pranks that I am in pain."

Parvati's explanation sobered Ganesha. He understood the grave responsibility of his mother which he also had to share. His mother Goddess Parvati was not just his mother. She mothered the entire existence. And she existed within the existence. If he caused pain to others, he caused her pain too. It was as simple as that.

He immediately regretted his acts and asked for forgiveness. Never again would he hurt another being for fun. Once Parvati forgave him, he said with soulful eyes, "Mother, I'm hungry."

Under no circumstances could he forget the modaks or suffer hunger pangs. Parvati gathered him in her arms and carried him to the modaks. She had hidden them away from his prying eyes to impart a valuable lesson.

Ganesha squealed in delight and carried away the entire tray!

Source – Ganesha Purana

6.
THE VANQUISHING OF GAJAMUKHASURA'S EGO AND HOW THE MOUSE BECAME GANESHA'S TRANSPORT

Ganesha had a very busy life indeed. Always rushing to resolve one calamity after another. There was absolutely no rest for him. Some demon, somewhere in creation, was always creating a disturbance for those in the mode of goodness. This time it was Gajamukhasura. There were some extra-smart demons who did not hesitate to do penance for thousands of years simply to please a god and receive a boon. The boon was always invincibility and immortality.

As Ganesha made his way to his destination, he wondered when the demons would understand that there were far more important things in life than power and deathlessness. Needless to say, Gajamukhasura had also attained a boon from Lord Shiva. That no weapon could kill him. Post the boon, he harassed devatas and *rishis* endlessly. He would even make them do 108 sit-ups three times a day! The devatas had complained to Lord Shiva, who had dispatched Ganesha to handle the matter. Although the demons thought they could defy death with their boons, the gods always had a trick up their sleeve.

Ganesha smiled. It would be fun this time. Although the demon could counter any weapon, Ganesha had weapons in his armour that would scare the daylights out of him. Now Ganesha started to chuckle. He could just imagine the demon's horrific expressions when his weapons were rendered useless by the power of Ganesha's weapons.

Soon, Gajamukhasura and Ganesha were face to face. The demon challenged the god in open defiance, spilling with the confidence of certain victory. Ganesha hurled his weapon to check how the demon would handle it. To his credit, the demon was quick in retaliating and nullifying it. Ganesha hurled one weapon after another and to his surprise none of them made any impact on the demon. Soon, he had exhausted all his weapons.

What should he do now? How to kill the demon without using a weapon?

There was no time to think because the demon was already roaring and advancing towards him, eager to finish his enemy. In an instant, Ganesha was enlightened by a thought. He touched his tusks. They were as efficient as weapons. Yet they were not weapons. In one jerk, he pulled out a tusk and it whizzed past to hit bang on target.

Gajamukhasura saw the tusk coming. He changed himself into a mouse to avoid being hit. All of a sudden, there was a loud noise and a dazzling explosion; a series of things happened and next thing he knew was that Ganesha was sitting on him. Instead of killing the demon, Ganesha had killed his ego. He cursed the demon to remain a mouse and the mouse humbly bowed to Ganesha, eager to serve him as his vehicle.

The power of Ganesha is such that he can crush even mountains of vanity and ego into the size of a mouse and use it for transport!

In another version it is said that Gajamukhasura had a pious wife, who was devoted to Goddess Gauri. She always kept Gauri *vrat* for the well-being of her husband. Thus, it became Gauri's responsibility to save the demon from Ganesha's attack. When Ganesha hurled his deadly tusk at him, Gauri held it back, unwilling to allow the tusk to reach its target. A startled Ganesha asked his mother why she was on his enemy's side, protecting him. As Gauri began to explain to her son the whole story, Ganesha's attention got diverted. Taking advantage of the distraction, Gajamukhasura jumped at the opportunity transforming himself into a mouse so small that he could escape from the scene. But Ganesha, who is always alert, jumped on the mouse and subjugated him, using him as his vehicle. The mouse came to be called Mooshak.

There's yet another belief about how the mouse came to be Ganesha's means of transportation.

Krauncha was a gandharva (musician-god) in the court of Indra. One day, he accidentally stepped on the toes of Sage Vamadeva. It was a mistake that could have been pardoned but for the sage, it was unpardonable—so much so that he cursed the gandharva and turned him into a mouse, much to the shock of Krauncha.

From a musician-god, Krauncha had now turned into a mouse! That too a mouse huge in size. As tall as a mountain. He ran here and there, but because of his size, he destroyed everything that came in his path. He just couldn't help it. Everything appeared so minuscule that even touching something led to destruction. Krauncha, in panic, ran and ran, not knowing what to do, where to go. His heart was beating so wildly that he feared it would pop out.

Running in a daze, he reached an ashram. It belonged to a learned sage, Parashar muni. Inevitably, he caused a lot of havoc there too, destroying the ashram itself unintentionally. Krauncha was confused and depressed. Suddenly he felt himself being dragged. Someone had thrown a noose around his neck and was pulling him. Krauncha was terrified. Someone wanted to kill him.

Finally, the pulling stopped. He could see the person's feet. He looked up to see the face of his attacker. It was not a demon or an enemy but Lord Ganesha. He sighed in relief as tension drained out of his body. Ganesha's kind face gave him comfort. He tried to focus to hear what he was saying.

"Krauncha, you have caused enough destruction here and everywhere else. If it was a demon, I would have punished him. But you are a gandharva. I know you are not doing this intentionally. So, I will make you small and use you as my vehicle. Is that ok?"

Ganesha's soft and soothing voice calmed Krauncha. His palpitations stopped. He nodded his head agreeing to whatever Ganesha was saying. After all, he was a friend. Soon he felt something weird happening to his body. He closed his eyes in distress. He could not handle any more shocks. Ganesha had shrunk his body so that he was now the size of a normal mouse. Ganesha then mounted his back. Krauncha felt himself being crushed to death. Horrified and unable to bear his massive weight, he squealed. "Ganesha, can you please reduce your weight? You're just too heavy!!"

Ganesha realised his mistake. No doubt, he did weigh a lot. Definitely too heavy for a mouse! For the sake of the mouse, he had to reduce his weight. He quickly made himself feather light so that Krauncha would be comfortable enough to support him.

And since then, Ganesha has been riding on the mouse because it helps him reach every corner of the world with great ease. Whether it's a tiny hole or a dark alley, his mouse and he can manoeuvre all paths and save the distressed.

Source – Ganesha Purana

7.
WHY THE MOON GOD IS PART OF ALL FASTING RITUALS

Ganesha's love for food was well-known. If food was anywhere around him, he could not control himself and would eat everything he could lay his hands on. Parvati pampered her little boy and gave him lots of laddus and modaks. But no matter how much he ate, he could never have enough of them. Imagine his ecstasy when one day, Kubera, the treasurer of the gods, invited everyone for a dinner banquet. He waited patiently for the appointed hour to arrive so that he could eat to his heart's (and stomach's) content.

Sure enough, he reached the banquet well on time. He felt a deep sense of contentment simply by looking at the inviting spread of laddus, modaks (dumplings filled with jaggery and coconut), and *barfis* of hundreds of varieties. There was modak dipped in jaggery sauce as well as honey coated. Barfis of fifty varieties. Unlimited laddus of variegated shapes, sizes, and colours. Some big, some small, some white, some yellow. Round, oval, heart shaped. Cinnamon flavoured, some kesar flavoured. He had to taste each and every one. Which he made sure he did!

Evening turned into late night when he finally decided to call it a day. But wait a minute! There were so many more laddus lying on the table begging him to eat more. He stroked his large pendulous abdomen. There was no place in there. His host suggested he pack some and take for his family as well. Ganesha jumped at the idea. He could continue the feast the next day as well. Smiling broadly, he gathered a rather large number of sweets in a bag. But his tummy had become so huge that walking became a bit difficult. If he could only make it to the exit, he would then climb onto his faithful Mooshak, the mouse carrier. Somehow, he staggered and rolled and plonked himself on Mooshak.

But there was a problem. Darkness had fallen and the timid mouse was scared to cross the dense forest. Even balancing Ganesha was a tough job, thanks to his weight. Ganesha kept falling sideways, forward, and backward. And then he burped. The burp was so violent that Mooshak trembled with the vibration and before he could realise what was happening, he stumbled on a rock and fell. Down came Ganesha with his laddus and all. Ouch! Ouch! Both Mooshak and Ganesha moaned as they lay sprawled on the ground on their backs. The bag of sweets too fell from his hands, spilling all the delicious sweets. Ganesha was acutely embarrassed. His size had increased so much that his poor mouse had tumbled under his weight.

He looked around hoping no one had seen this sight. How humiliating it would be to be laughed upon. Thankfully, there was no one nearby. He sighed with relief and gratitude. His dhoti was torn but his dignity was intact. Just as he was gathering himself to rise, he heard the faint sound of suppressed laughter. As if someone wanted to burst out laughing but was trying to control it. Afraid, he looked around. No one was in sight. Then he looked up. He saw the moon god, with his hands covering his mouth, chuckling softly. So, he's the one laughing at me, thought Ganesha.

The least the moon god could have done was come down and helped him, thought Ganesha whose pride (more than bones) was injured by the moon god. When he continued to glare up the sky at Chandrama with looks that could kill, Chandrama thought he had better explain himself.

"O' Ganesha, you look so funny fallen on the ground with your huge potbelly and small feet. How will the little mouse carry a huge weight like yours?"

To Ganesha's chagrin, now the jocund Chandrama was not even suppressing his glee but laughing out aloud wholeheartedly. Ganesha didn't like this at all. At all! He hated being laughed at. He stood up quicker than expected with his bulky form and gave Chandrama a piece of his mind.

"So, you think I look funny, and you are handsome? Is that right, Mr. Handsome? How proud you are of your good looks. But the whole world knows that this beauty is not yours; it is borrowed. It is sunlight that you reflect which gives you this glow."

Ganesha, in fury, decided that Chandrama deserved a severe dressing down and punishment. He extracted his tusk and tossed it high aiming at him. The tusk hit the moon hard making a depression on him. The impression was so deep that it was visible from the earth and became what we now know as a crater. But this did not suffice to ease Ganesha's monumental distress.

"I curse you that henceforth, sunlight will not fall on you, and you will become invisible to the world. You will have no beauty to be proud of."

Only after uttering these harsh words did Ganesha calm down. Now it was Chandrama's turn to writhe in agony. He immediately stepped down from the sky to pacify the agitated elephant god.

"O' Ganesha. I was only joking. Please forgive me for hurting your feelings. Do not curse me to a life of invisibility."

By then Ganesha had calmed down and he realised he had unnecessarily cursed him. Chandrama was truly repentant. So was Ganesha. Although he could not take back a curse that was already pronounced, he could definitely modify it.

"Since the curse is not reversible," he said, "you will lose your weight in a cyclic manner for fourteen days, become invisible only for one day, and put on weight again in the next fourteen days. Thus, it is only one day that you will be invisible. And because today is Chaturthi, it will be an inauspicious act to look at you on a Chaturthi. Whoever does so will get stuck with unnecessary false allegations and troubles. I also declare that no worship will be complete without seeing your face first. Only after your *darshan* can devotees eat and break the fast."

A relieved moon god folded his hands in gratitude and went back to the sky, glad that he had not lost his identity in totality. And that is why sometimes the moon shines bright and sometimes the night is dark. And that is also why the moon is an important part of all fasting rituals.

Source – Ganesha Purana

8.
VIGHNAHARTA GANESHA AND THE COMPETITION

Never had the heavenly planets seen so much excitement. The demigods were bubbling with excitement after the celestial announcement. Lord Shiva had announced a competition for all demigods who wanted to take part in it. The announcement had been triggered by the need to appoint one demigod who could be considered the first one to be worshipped to help overcome obstacles. Also, the worship of that demigod would be auspicious to start a new venture. Thus, the winner of the competition would be awarded that status.

No wonder the heavens were beehives of activity. Everyone was discussing the various possibilities while harbouring the desire for that coveted position.

The terms of the competition had not been announced. The heavenly residents waited with anticipatory anxiety as to what would be required from them. Would it be something as simple as displaying their yogic powers or would it be a physical challenge? Or perhaps a measure of intellectual capacity? One guess was as good as another, and the suspense ended with the final announcement.

Lord Shiva's husky voice boomed across the heavenly horizon.

"May I have your attention, citizens of heaven? I place before you a task. The winner of the task shall be designated to hold the post of being the first to be remembered by mortals on earth. The task is to circle the whole world thrice and whoever is the winner will be appointed to the post."

There was an uproar amongst the demigods now. Circling the world was a test of speed. Those who had fast vehicles were thrilled while those with mediocre vehicles were busy thinking about how to accelerate. Those like Ganesha who had a mouse for a vehicle did not want to participate at all. Moreover, Ganesha was not even interested in this contest.

Everyone gathered at the appointed hour for the historical event. This was something they would remember forever and would pass down generation after generation. It was the largest gathering of demigods ever.

Indra came on his mighty elephant. Durga was on her ferocious lion. Shani arrived on his crow and Kartikeya on his peacock. Yamaraj sported his buffalo and Saraswati her swan. A murmur of dissent went up in the air when Aditya arrived on his seven horses.

The commotion intensified with the arrival of Vayu on his thousand horses! And everyone burst into a merry laughter when Ganesha too took his position at the start line mounted on his tiny mouse. He laughed with them because he knew it was funny. He had no chance of winning whatsoever but he didn't care about winning. He only wanted to participate for the fun of it and it was a fabulous opportunity to travel around the world too. Maybe someone would offer him a plateful of modaks or two. That would definitely make his day!

The race began. All participants whizzed past Ganesha putting in their best efforts. Ganesha was lagging behind right from the start. What was the hurry? He would take his own sweet time and enjoy the journey. As he was hovering somewhere between two planets, he saw Narada muni watching the demigods rush past him. No one had the time to stop and greet him. Ganesha, however, was always eager to meet the wise Narada and gather pearls of wisdom from him. What could be better than a chance encounter with the saintly Narada?

Bursting with enthusiasm, Ganesha went closer to Narada muni and greeted him humbly with folded hands.

"My dear Ganesha!" Narada exclaimed with joy, "what a pleasure to see you! What is going on? Why are all these exalted demigods rushing? Where are they going and why are they in so much of a hurry?" enquired the sage.

"Oh Narada muni, haven't you heard? There's a competition . . . a race to go around the world. The winner will be given the special post of being the god of honour for all auspicious beginnings. He will be the one who will be worshipped as the remover of all obstacles."

"I see." Narada reflected on this and said, "No wonder all the demigods ignored me . . . no one wanted to stop and greet me lest they get delayed. They even avoided looking at me."

Ganesha felt sad for Narada muni. He said, "I know I can't win the race, but I wanted to travel around the world. I'm glad I did because I bumped into you. You're such a treasure trove of wisdom. It is my good fortune to have your association."

Heartfelt words always make an impact and Narada muni was touched by Ganesha's sensitivity. He wanted to help Ganesha somehow. He was the only one who had stopped to greet him. The others had forgotten all etiquette in their thirst for a position. Only Ganesha had given more importance to respect, and he deserved to win. Thinking hard about how he could help, he suddenly had a brilliant idea.

Beaming broadly, he said to Ganesha, "Dear child, would you like to win? I can tell you how."

Ganesha was zapped. How could he ever win on a mouse? He looked at his mouse and then at the sage. Narada muni leaned towards him and whispered in his ear.

"Please go back to Kailash and write the name Rama there and circle it thrice. The holy name of Rama contains the whole world. That is all you need to do. You will then win the contest."

Ganesha's eyes popped out with Narada muni's radical plan. He thanked him profusely and rushed back to Kailash. On his way back he bumped into many demigods who laughed at him thinking he was giving up the race. But ignoring them, he reached Kailash where his parents were. They were surprised to see him back so soon. They were even more surprised to see him write 'Rama' on the ground.

"What are you doing son?" Parvati asked lovingly. They knew he could not win the race, so they did not ask about it.

Ganesha did not reply. He quietly continued with writing and then he drew a circle around it. Next, he folded his hands and walked along the circle three times very gravely.

His parents were still staring at him unable to fathom his strange actions. Finally, on completing the triple circumambulation, he said, "I have circled the world thrice because I have learnt from you that nothing is bigger than the holy name of Rama and this name means the world to all of us. So, I am back after circling my world thrice."

Wow! Lord Shiva jumped up from his asana and hugged Ganesha tightly with love and pride.

"I'm so proud of you, my son."

He looked at Parvati. She nodded, giving assent to his desire of declaring him the winner.

"I declare you the winner of the race!" said an ecstatic Shiva.

This is how Ganesha was selected for the position and as we all know, Ganesha is known as Vighnaharta and worshipped first and foremost for an auspicious beginning of new projects.

Source – Folk Tales

9.

HOW GANESHA GOT THE NICKNAME MAYURESHWAR

Queen Ugra, happy that she had conceived, had no idea what was in store for her. For the moment she was revelling in her long overdue pregnancy. A lot of sacrificing had been done to be blessed with the baby. To the extent of severe penance to please the sun god. And it had paid off. The sun god did bless her and fulfilled her wishes. However, she was not prepared for what was to follow.

The embryo within her was so powerful and effulgent that it was outside her capacity to hold on to it. Her body was scorched by his brilliance and the discomfort became so unbearable that she had to simply get it out. Who could possibly hold on to fire? Thinking that the ocean was the best place, she released the embryo in the soothing waters of the Lord of the ocean.

Samudra devata took custody of the child and then went to the king's court and handed the child back to the king and the queen. Since he was born from the ocean, he was named Sindhu.

Shukracharya, Sindhu's guru, had very high ambitions for him. He sent Sindhu to perform a penance to please the sun god so as to become more powerful. Thus, obeying the instructions of his guru, Sindhu performed austerities for two thousand years, meditating on Lord Surya. Surya finally appeared before him ready to grant him a boon.

"If you are pleased with me, please grant me the boon of immortality," said Sindhu.

Surya gave him the boon with drops of nectar. "Take this nectar and drink it. As long as the nectar is around your navel, you will not die. No one can kill you." Then he disappeared in a flash, as quickly as he had appeared leaving behind a dazed and elated Sindhu.

What does one do after getting a boon like that? Of course, he sets out to show off his powers and control others. That's what Sindhu wanted too. More power and more control. He took over all the planets including the heavens. He defeated Lord Indra and usurped his throne. It gave him great joy to imprison all the gods in his kingdom while he ruled over heaven. Only one place was left. Or so he thought. And that place was Mount Kailash. That's what every demon had believed before their end was near.

He decided to conquer this one last kingdom and then declare himself the undisputed supremo of the universe. When the gods learnt of the demon's wicked plan, they all began a *yagya.* A yagya to invoke and worship Ganesha. No one but Ganesha could help them out of this calamity. He was intelligent and resourceful, and no demon could ever think of defeating Ganesha. With a prayer in their hearts, they started the fire sacrifice.

Ganesha always rushes to those who need him. Soon he was standing amongst the gods listening to them about their plight. He heard about Sindhu's atrocities and his quest for power. Knowing that it was an urgent matter, he assured them that he would take birth as the son of Parvati and kill the demon. Ganesha's words were like cooling moon rays on the scorched and blazing hearts of the gods.

Meanwhile, Parvati had been immersed in penance for twelve years on a mountain as suggested by Shiva. The penance was to attain a child who would be as virtuous and powerful as her husband Lord Shiva. Vishnu soon made an appearance, looking resplendent in his jewelled ornaments. Seated over Shesha in *padmasan*, Lord Vishnu assured Parvati that she would soon be blessed with a son.

On the bright fourth day of Bhadrapada, in Swati constellation, Ganesha arrived bearing six arms, three eyes, and a beautiful nose. His body, as lustrous as a thousand suns, very obviously announced to Shiva and Parvati that he was not an ordinary child but someone special.

Days passed and soon Ganesha was ten years old. He prepared to attack Sindhu in his Ganduki nagar as per his commitment to the gods. Hearing the news, Sindhu sent Kamalasura to stop Ganesha in his tracks. But they were like small wasps for the mighty Ganesha. Next, Sindhu sent his two sons to deal with the attack, but Ganesha easily finished off the two novices. In a hurry to kill Sindhu, he did not waste any time on other obstacles in his way.

When he heard the news of the death of his powerful sons, Sindhu fled in fear. He had known that only Ganesha could kill him. Panic set in as his father advised him to surrender to Ganesha, but the egoistic demon preferred to escape rather than bow down before anyone. The tables had suddenly turned. It was now Sindhu running instead of the gods. Ganesha was hot on his heels and soon caught up with him. If he had to be killed, it was necessary to remove the nectar from around the demon's navel. Using his weapon Parshu (axe), Ganesha removed the nectar from Sindhu's navel and in one clean swoop, he killed him.

Like a tree that refuses to bend in a storm and thus falls on the ground, Sindhu too fell flat. His ego and power hunger had spelled his end.

Since Ganesha was on a peacock for this mission, he earned himself the nickname 'Mayureshwar'.

Ganesha comes on different vehicles in different yugas.

While in Satya yuga, he mounts a lion and is born to Sage Kashyapa and Aditi, in Treta yuga he is on the peacock with Shiva and Parvati as his parents. In Satya yuga he had ten arms and was red-complexioned while in Treta yuga he sported six arms and a white complexion. At the end of Treta yuga he gives his peacock to his brother Skanda. In Satya yuga he kills the demons Narantaka and Devanataka as well as Dhumraksha while in Treta yuga, he comes to end the tyranny of Sindhu. In Dwapar yuga, he uses the mouse as his vehicle and is again born to Shiva and Parvati as Gajanan. He is pink-complexioned and annihilates the demon Sindura. In this incarnation he speaks the *Ganesha Gita* to King Varenya. In Kali yuga, *Bhavishya Purana* says he will appear as a grey-complexioned Dhumraketu with two or four arms and mounting a horse.

Source – Ganesha Purana

10. HOW BABY GANESHA CONQUERED THE DEMON SINDHU

Sindhu, a demon, had spent all his life terrorising people. Now it was his turn to live in terror. He had heard that Ganesha had taken birth as Gajanan for the sole purpose of killing him. The cowardly gods had requested him to help them, and he had arrived. Gods were a big nuisance in Sindhu's life. The only way out was to nip the new menace in the bud. It would be much easier to kill baby Ganesha rather than allow his powers to grow with him.

The solution was so simple he laughed out aloud. Yes, he would make sure Ganesha died as a baby. He was five months old and that was old enough to die. The thought comforted him immensely and he relaxed, convinced that Ganesha was as good as dead.

He mobilised his demonic army and told them to attack Ganesha in succession till he died. The first to take up the challenge was a demon in the form of a vulture. It would be easy for a strong vulture to make mincemeat of a child. Or so he thought.

The demon flew to Parvati's courtyard where Ganesha was playing. He swooped down and caught Ganesha in his beak. Ganesha loved birds and excitedly hung on to his beak in a playful manner. He didn't make a single sound, afraid that his mother would come and forbid him to play with strangers. And that too a bird as vicious as a vulture. So, he quietly played along. The vulture held him in his beak and in a flash, soared high up into the sky. One moment Ganesha was there playing and the next moment, he was gone. In the blink of an eye.

But Parvati was always alert. She immediately noticed the absence of her precious darling and raised an alarm. She called out to Ganesha, thinking he may be playing hide and seek with her. Unable to spot him and in a panic, her eyes wandered up to the sky to see her Ganesha dangling from the beak of a vulture. She nearly lost her breath at the bizarre sight. How would she reach him there to save him?

Ganesha looked down to see his mother frantically calling out to him. He had never seen her so disturbed. Not wanting to cause any further distress to her, he decided to end his playtime. He simply punched the bird, and the bird was knocked out. In a freefall, the vulture and Ganesha both landed back on the ground. Parvati dashed to pick up her beloved son and kissed him, relieved to find him unharmed. The vulture however lay dead. She had no idea how and why the vulture came but she didn't care. Fondling her son, she vowed to keep a closer eye on him.

Unknown to her, the next demon was already on the way to her house. This time she made Ganesha sleep next to her in a cradle as she went around doing her chores. The next thing she knew was that there were two horrible smelling demons bent over her son. Before she could come to his aid, Ganesha had kicked them hard breaking their bodies. Blood oozed out of their wounds, and they dissolved in thin air. An aghast Parvati froze where she was, as if watching an action-packed movie.

Parvati soon realised that there was no place safe for her son. She could only intensify her vigil and make sure he was always under her protection. Because her baby needed to be protected. Such are the beliefs of mothers. The next day when an ascetic's son came to play with Ganesha, she did not mind. But the boy soon pinned Ganesha down and tried to kill him. Ganesha hit back and Parvati thought Ganesha was trying to kill a brahman boy. She tried to intervene in the fight to save the boy but the sagely boy transformed into a dark devil. Again, Ganesha caught him and killed him. Horrified, Parvati picked up her son to keep him at a safe distance away from the demon. What if the demon resurrected himself?

Thankfully, he didn't. But another one took his place. Vyoma, a very notorious demon, perched himself on the highest branch of a tree outside their courtyard. Ganesha usually loved to play under the shade of that tree. As soon as Ganesha came to play, he shook the tree so violently that it created a storm of dust and leaves. The entire vicinity, including Ganesha's house, was covered by that storm. Nothing was visible to anyone. Parvati was momentarily blinded.

Taking advantage of the temporary cover, the demon attacked Ganesha. However, when the storm settled down, Ganesha was still playing blissfully under the tree while the demon lay soaked in blood nearby. No one knew what had transpired. Parvati was just grateful that Ganesha had survived the ordeal.

When Vyoma's sister heard about her brother's gory death, she trembled in rage. Her specialty was that she could devour anyone, no matter how brave or huge. She vowed to devour Ganesha and extract revenge. Coming up with a novel idea, she disguised herself as a beautiful young teenager in distress and took shelter of Parvati. Out of compassion, Parvati gave her food and shelter for the night in her own room.

Ganesha was quite aware of the intentions of their guest. In the middle of the night, the demoness approached Ganesha's cradle. Ganesha playfully caught hold of her nose and ears. What apparently seemed like a child's playful act was a deathly gesture because his hands were not soft like those of an infant but as hard as iron. It was impossible for the attacker to wriggle out of his solid grip as he continued to squeeze her hard. Like a thunderbolt, his iron grip sucked the breath out of her. Not realising what was going on, Parvati's attendants rushed to save the guest. But they could not do anything other than look helplessly at Ganesha's systematic destruction of the demoness. Finally, the wicked girl fell on the ground breathing her last. A gleeful Ganesha, who was still in his cradle, clapped as if his toy had fallen out of his hands.

In this way, Ganesha foiled all attempts of Sindhu to kill him and forced Sindhu to come and fight with Ganesha himself.

Source – Ganesha Purana

11.
GANESHA – THE PLAYFUL FOODIE

It was a beautiful evening. A gentle breeze was blowing and flowers danced gleefully. Little Ganesha was inspired to go after the colourful butterflies that were hopping from flower to flower. He tried to catch them as the butterflies teased him and stayed out of his reach. Hours passed in this exciting sport accompanied by his friends.

Soon Ganesha and his friends found themselves in strange surroundings. Where were they? They had no clue. Deeply engrossed in playing with butterflies, the children had ventured into unknown territories and were lost! If they had not been so immersed in chasing the butterflies, they would have never taken the risk. What now? Not only were they lost but their stomachs were growling in hunger, threatening to collapse if not fed.

Ganesha's friends gathered around him, complaining of unbearable hunger. Ganesha's stomach was rumbling too. They plucked on some berries but what were a few berries for the growling stomachs of foodies? It did not feel like they had eaten anything at all. Suddenly they heard the ringing of bells and chanting of shlokas. They deduced that an *arti* was happening nearby, which meant surely there was an ashram in the vicinity.

Enthused by the knowledge, they followed the tinkling of the bell. Sure enough, they found themselves in the courtyard of Gautama rishi's ashram and a mouth-watering aroma drifting from the kitchen hit their noses. Unable to control himself any longer, Ganesha, as if in a trance, followed the delicious calling. He loved food and nothing could come in between him and food.

He turned back to signal his friends to wait where they were. If too many entered, there were high chances of being caught. Besides, Ganesha alone was enough to carry ample food in his trunk. As he tiptoed towards the kitchen, he saw Gautama rishi performing a yagya. He stood on his toes to peep into the kitchen to see mother Ahalya cooking a wide variety of dishes. Smacking his lips, he waited for her to leave.

Ahalya was already late that day in putting together the meal and she did not want to be the cause of the delay for her husband's rituals. She hurried out to inform him that the meal was ready. Exit mother Ahalya. Enter naughty Ganesha.

Once inside the kitchen, he whistled to his friends to come outside the window. They came running, filled with anticipation for a feast and they were not disappointed. Ganesha handed them dish after dish of exotic, heavenly, ghee- and sugar-laden goodies. Finally, Ganesha jumped out and joined his friends carrying the last bowl with him.

They ran into the safety of the woods again where they could gobble down their booty. Meanwhile, unaware of what had transpired in the kitchen behind her back, Ahalya had gone to inform Gautama rishi that he could take the cooked food from the kitchen.

But when the rishi entered the kitchen, he saw the kitchen strangely empty. Annoyed at Ahalya, he called out to her, "Is this a joke? There's nothing in the kitchen. What am I supposed to offer and eat?"

Puzzled, Ahalya returned to show him the lovely dishes she had prepared for him. Her eyes opened wide to see there was absolutely nothing there. Nothing! Zilch! Nada! Where could all the food have disappeared? The two of them realised something fishy was going on. Outside the window, there were some remnants of the food that had been cooked. Obviously, someone had come and stolen it from their ashram. Alarmed at such a theft, which had never happened in their life before, they followed the food trail.

It led them out of the ashram and into the woods. To their surprise they saw the young band of robbers relishing the hearty meal. The culprits had been caught red-handed.

"How naughty can you be, Ganesha? Son of Shiva, stealing food from other people's houses? How shameful!" chided mother Ahalya.

"He and his friends need to be taught a lesson," continued Gautama rishi as he dragged him by his ears to take him to mother Parvati so that she knew what her brat was up to.

Little Ganesha hung his head and walked behind the rishi, unable to understand what the big deal was if he just took some food to feed his and his friends' stomach. Since when had eating become a crime? Sometimes he found it impossible to understand adults. They tended to complicate everything. Even eating. He vowed to be a more sensible adult in the future. And more compassionate with those who loved eating.

But for now, he had to face the drama unfurling in front of him. When Parvati heard what her son had done, she was extremely embarrassed. She hadn't expected Ganesha to rob others' houses. Agreed, he had a huge appetite. Agreed, he was pampered. But robbing was simply not acceptable. She promised Gautama rishi she would punish Ganesha adequately for his misdeed, all the while apologising profusely.

Satisfied with her assurances, Gautama rishi left. But he left behind one very angry mother. Parvati now chastised Ganesha for spoiling the family name and reputation and then tied him to his bed with a rope.

Ganesha cried at his mother's harsh words and punishment. He hated being tied up like a wild animal. It was inhuman actually. But he had no say in the matter. Parvati left a crying Ganesha and went to do her chores. When she emerged after completing her chores, she saw Ganesha playing in the courtyard.

Puzzled, she went inside her room and saw Ganesha tied up there the way she had left him. She sat a while to calm herself and she felt Ganesha sitting in her lap. She glanced across and saw Ganesha still tied to the bed. Something very weird was going on.

Baffled, she went to visit Gautama rishi to apologise to him again. But Ahalya assured her that she should forget about it now. But there too, she saw Ganesha playing. She went to him and said, "Ganesha, let's go home."

The children said, "Mother, Ganesha is not here. He is at home."

Now Parvati could see Ganesha crying. And then laughing. And then eating. She was seeing Ganesha everywhere. Parvati ran home and found Ganesha still tied up and crying. She untied him and hugged him tightly. Then she fed him his favourite food with her own hands.

Back at the ashram, Gautama rishi was also feeling guilty that he had complained about the innocent boy who had only eaten out of hunger. So Ahalya made the choicest of dishes for Ganesha and his friends and went and gave them to Ganesha.

Ganesha was happy now, although he still couldn't understand adults. But as long as he was surrounded by his favourite foods, he didn't really care.

Source – Ganesha Purana

12.
KARTHIKEYA'S WEDDING

On a bright sunny morning at his home in Kailash Mountain, Ganesha laughed heartily at his brother Kartikeya's love story. Kartikeya was head over heels in love and the thought delighted Ganesha to no end. Again and again, he asked Kartikeya to repeat what he wanted from him. Big brother Kartikeya needed little brother Ganesha's help to get married to the love of his life. And little brother was more than willing to help him out. But to begin with, he wanted to extract as much pleasure he could by pulling big brother's legs.

"Tell me again exactly what happened," squealed Ganesha.

And Kartikeya began his long story once again.

"A few years ago, I had been constantly bombarded with prayers from the chief of a mountain tribe in South India to grant him a child. Pleased with his sincere prayers, I bestowed him with a baby girl. The couple named her Valli. Valli reached adolescence and looked like an angel; she had long black hair till her waist, her eyes shone with the goodness of her . . ."

When Kartikeya stopped mid-sentence, Ganesha knew he was in a trance, once again. Kartikeya was staring ahead with a blank expression, as if he had forgotten to breathe while lost in his thoughts. Ganesha nudged him to bring him back to the present.

"Like her parents, she too was devoted to me—Lord Murugan. Moved by her fervent desire to attain me, one day I appeared in a millet field where she was tending to the crops. I introduced myself as a tribal hunter who had lost his way while hunting. My well-toned body and dreamy looks should have surely captured her heart. But before I could make any conversation with her, her brothers arrived. Not wanting to arouse their suspicions and complicate matters, I turned myself into a tree. They had brought fruits and honey for her to eat. After they left, I changed back to my disguised form. Looking into her deep eyes, I proposed to her . . ."

Ganesha saw Kartikeya's cheeks turn a crimson red, embarrassed to reveal his heart. Ganesha nodded, urging him to continue.

"Valli had no idea that the tribal hunter proposing to her was her beloved Murugan himself. In her ignorance, she refused my hand and spat angry words at me. Before I had a chance to speak further, I saw her brothers returning. I think they must have seen her talking to me . . . I had to think fast, and I immediately disguised myself as an old man. The brothers told me to take care of Valli till they returned from their hunting expedition."

Ganesha was holding his stomach with both hands and laughing hysterically now; his brother had been acting like a love-sick puppy. Kartikeya threw angry glances at Ganesha hoping to stop him from embarrassing him further. He really needed his brother's help and so he continued to ignore Ganesha's jovial bantering.

"Valli then gave me some millets and honey to eat which I accepted and ate gracefully. Next, I felt thirsty, so she went and brought water for me from a stream nearby. I remarked jokingly that my thirst for water was quenched but my thirst for a companion remained. She did not like this comment at all and now I'm afraid I've lost her forever. Unless you help me."

Ganesha could not possibly refuse his brother's request for help. He had helped gods and sages all his life and when it came to his own brother, he would stop at nothing.

He said to Kartikeya, "Brother, all your worries are now my worries. Tomorrow go back and meet her and I will make sure that she accepts your proposal."

Ganesha's confident attitude imparted hope to Kartikeya and his face lit up with a smile. He embraced Ganesha, squeezing him tight. "I owe you bro," he whispered into his ears.

Kartikeya was back in the field dressed as an old man. Ganesha followed him carrying a foolproof plan with him. He transformed himself into a massive white elephant with tusks as menacing as a warrior's sword. He came charging across the fields, as mad elephants would, destroying the crops that came in his way. Seeing the ruckus created by the mad elephant, Valli froze in fear. She had nowhere to hide. Sweat dripped down her brows and she imagined the outcome of being trampled by the rogue elephant. The only person around was the old man. She ran towards him like a river rushing to merge with the ocean; flinging her arms around him and yelling at the top of her voice to help her. The old man was quick to pounce on the opportunity provided by Ganesha and proposed to protect her in exchange for her hand in marriage.

Wanting to save her life at any cost, the tribal princess agreed. She had only to agree when the elephant disappeared, and the old man transformed himself into the young Lord Kartikeya. When Valli saw the transformation, her heart skipped a beat as her eyes gazed at the divine beauty of her Lord Murugan whom she had fervently prayed for on a regular basis. It was her beloved Lord showing his *lilas*.

She ran into his embrace and soon it became a ritual for Valli and Kartikeya to spend long loving hours together in the field, lost in their own world. When Valli's father heard that his daughter was in love with an old man, he lost his temper.

Furious with the treachery of the old man, father and brothers marched into the field, determined to put an end to this inappropriate saga. They shot arrows at the old man but to their consternation, none of the arrows even touched him. Every arrow fell short of the target and dissipated into thin air halfway across. Not only were their arrows ineffective, but the father and brothers themselves dropped dead miraculously.

The dead bodies of her family evoked piteous cries from Valli. She ran towards them in a desperate attempt to revive them. Shaking them and begging them to get up, she sank into total despair. She then ran back to Kartikeya and pleaded with him to bring her family back to life.

Kartikeya had no intention of harming her family. He gently instructed her to go and touch them and with the touch of her fingers they would be revived to life again. Not fully convinced, she touched them. One by one they all came back from the dead. A big chaos followed with everyone talking and no one listening.

It was an unbelievable experience for the whole family. There were celebrations galore and an opulent wedding befitting a god. Ganesha proudly accompanied his brother and ensured a smooth wedding.

Source – Folk Tales

13.

GANESHA'S WEDDING WITH SIDDHI AND RIDDHI

Mount Kailash was bathed in golden sun rays that caressed the snow creating a dazzling effect. Everything shone like gold that day in the sparkling abode of Lord Shiva and his family. Both his children, his pride, were now grown up and had expressed their desire to get married. The question was—who would be the first to tie the knot? It was a difficult decision for Shiva choosing one over the other, but Parvati had come to his rescue. She always did. Shiva looked at her affectionately as she came up with a simple solution. She said they had to prove their worth in a competition. The faster one to circle thrice around the entire universe would be married first. Surprisingly, the boys agreed to the condition.

Surprising, because there was no way Ganesha could win such a competition on his vehicle, a mouse. Kartikeya had a peacock to mount on . . . definitely faster than the mouse. While Kartikeya's face lit up at the terms of the contest, Ganesha put on a brave face and sportingly agreed. Not once did it occur to him to negotiate the deal. Shiva mentally appreciated Ganesha's innocence and blessed him.

What happened next amazed both Shiva and Parvati. It made them realise they had a gem of a son. He knew very well that he had no chance of defeating Kartikeya on his mouse. So, he came up with a brilliant plan. He circled his parents thrice, with folded hands. When a shocked Parvati asked him why he wasn't going around the world, the clever Ganesha replied, "My universe is made up of my parents. By circumambulating my parents, I have gone around the world."

Ganesha's logic made perfect sense. How could they refute it? Neither did they want to. After accepting his argument, they simply waited for

Kartikeya to return. And he did, after a long, long wait. His jaw dropped to see Ganesha already there.

"Oh, did you not participate at all? Did you give up even before you began?" he enquired jokingly.

When he learnt how Ganesha had won the race, he too showed the same acceptance and sporting attitude that Ganesha had shown before.

For Ganesha, winning the race was easy. The more difficult task was to find a bride. Try as they did, no one wanted an elephant-headed groom. Time ticked by and he remained unmarried. It was especially difficult for Ganesha. His frustration mounted day by day. How long the wait would be, no one knew. Handling rejection is never easy.

Then one day, Ganesha heard that a devata was getting married. Something snapped inside him, and he decided to take revenge on anyone getting married. He gathered his resources, mainly his mouse Mooshak, and hatched a plan with him. Mooshak was his partner in crime.

What the two conspirators did was extreme but hilarious. The devious plan was that Mooshak would gather his cronies and together they would burrow many holes in the path of the marriage procession.

This would make walking difficult for everyone. Ganesha had a hearty laugh when he saw the guests and the groom tripping and falling all the way.

This went on for many a procession till the entire devata community realised it was Ganesha who was adamant about creating difficulties for them in every marriage. No one wanted to participate in marriage processions anymore fearing the difficult terrain. And all this because his marriage was not on the cards. Putting their heads together to solve the problem, the devatas came up with a plan. If only they could find a suitable alliance for Ganesha then perhaps he would stop this mischief. They escalated the matter and went to Lord Brahma. Brahma could easily create a girl who would marry Ganesha.

Lord Brahma readily agreed to solve all of Ganesha's blues. Born from Brahma were not one but two brides for Ganesha—Riddhi and Siddhi. Riddhi represented wealth and opulence. Siddhi represented intelligence and spiritual prowess. One is incomplete without the other. Riddhi without Siddhi is worthless. Likewise, Siddhi without Riddhi is futile. So, both were suitable brides for the unique bridegroom Ganesha. He could finally get married.

And he did. And he had two sons. Shubha and Labha. Auspiciousness and Profit. And a daughter Santoshi. Satisfaction, indeed!

Shiva Purana gives us another version of Ganesha's marriage. Riddhi and Siddhi were daughters of King Prajapati. The king had searched high and low and finally settled upon Kartikeya as his son-in-law. But the girls had a mind of their own. Their heart was captured by none other than the elephant-headed Ganesha. They would marry no one else but him. The king had no option but to send a proposal for Ganesha and in this way Riddhi and Siddhi became the consorts of Ganesha.

Ganesha bestows both these blessings on his devotees—wealth and intelligence. Ganesha shows us the way to achieve both intellect and prosperity because both are needed to have a meaningful life.

Source – Ganesha Purana

14.
HOW GANESHA CAME TO BE KNOWN AS LAMBODAR

Lord Shiva and Goddess Parvati sometimes held long discussions which went on for hours. Parvati loved to hear Lord Shiva speak to her about philosophical subjects like the chakra of life where Shiva explained about the laws of karma, life, and death. These were rare occasions as Shiva spent most of his time meditating on his Lord. And even when he was not meditating, he had a lot of visitors. And often, he would have to rush out of their home in Kailash to help others in distress. The few moments they had together were very valuable to both.

Parvati was waiting in anticipation for Lord Shiva to open his eyes so that she could request him to sit with her for a discussion. It had been many days since he had been immersed in samadhi and she was expecting him to be out of it soon. She wanted to be there in front of him when he came back to the external world before someone else got his attention. If she was not alert, she would be bereft of his association because word would spread that Shiva was now in external consciousness and a long queue of visitors would line up immediately. So, she sat at his feet, waiting for him to open his eyes.

Sure enough, Shiva soon spoke to her.

"Parvati," he exclaimed, "why are you sitting here?"

"Lord Shiva!" Parvati burst out in joy, "I've been waiting for you."

"Why?"

"I want to speak to you about the cycle of life and death. I want to know more about how one comes out of the karmic cycle. Last time we could not finish the discussion."

Lord Shiva smiled indulgently. Parvati was a sincere student and he loved her for that. He knew that soon he would have to attend to other duties so now was the best time to fulfil her desire to discuss.

In fact, he did not want to be disturbed till they had discussed to their heart's content. So, he called Ganesha and instructed him.

"Son, your mother and I have important matters to discuss. Can you please make sure that no one enters the gates of Kailash till we are done? I repeat, absolutely no one can be allowed inside! We do not want any interruptions."

Ganesha was happy to serve his parents. He would allow absolutely no one to enter their home. This was family time and that really made him glow with joy and pride.

Luckily for him, no one knew that Shiva was out of his meditation and so there were no visitors. But the peace and quiet was short-lived. People somehow smell facts, and news spread in the heavenly planets that Shiva was talking to Parvati. Indra heard the news too. Rather, this was the news he was waiting for quite anxiously. He had urgent business to discuss with him as he was again facing danger from fierce demons. He immediately gathered the heavenly devatas and proceeded to Kailash. The sooner they could meet Lord Shiva, the sooner he could solve their problem.

But haste makes waste. Their desire for a quick audience with Lord Shiva was left unmet. At the gates, they encountered Ganesha on an unusual duty. How could Ganesha allow them to enter when he had received instructions against it?

"Lord Indra, please stop. You cannot meet father now. He will not see anyone."

Indra did not like this unnecessary obstruction in his way. Never had anyone stopped him from entering Kailash. As far as he could remember, he had not been stopped from entering anywhere for that matter. He was Indra, Lord Indra! People welcomed him with open arms. Where was the question of being stopped?

Unable to control his anger, he snapped at Ganesha.

"What do you think you are doing? How can you stop us from meeting Lord Shiva? We have to discuss urgent business—our lives are at stake here," he said pointing out to all the devatas behind him who nodded in unison.

Ganesha heard him patiently and again repeated his instructions.

"I'm sorry, Lord Indra. You cannot meet father now. He will not see anyone."

Indra's temper now escalated, his anger inversely proportional to Ganesha's composure. Turning as red as vermillion, he was ready to attack if necessary.

When Ganesha continued to ignore his pleas, he declared war.

Ganesha prepared for war as that was the only way to keep Indra at bay. Indra, eager to meet Shiva, lost all sense of time as he engaged himself in a fierce battle with the powerful Ganesha.

Ganesha had no trouble in defeating Indra. But all his troubles started after that. He had put so much energy into fighting that after the hand-to-hand combat ended, he felt exhausted and weak. He never ever skipped eating but thanks to Indra's ego, he had foregone many meals. That had sapped all his energy. He looked around and finding a heap of fruits, he pounced upon them. One after another, he kept eating and eating. His hunger was at peak, and he couldn't stop gulping down every fruit and berry that came in front of his eyes.

After he felt a bit replenished and rejuvenated, he gulped down umpteen gallons of juices and water. With all the food tucked in his stomach, his stomach had become rather fat and round and was protruding out. He wondered if this was what people called a potbelly. Not that he cared. A round stomach only meant he had eaten well.

However, when Lord Shiva saw him and his potbelly, he burst into peals of laughter. He laughed so much that he was holding his stomach. Ganesha's huge belly was just too much. As he laughed, he kept shouting, "Lambodar, Lambodar," while pointing to his stomach.

Lambodar meant 'such a huge stomach' as *udar* means stomach. Since then, Ganesha is also known as Lambodar, a name lovingly gifted to him by his own father.

Source – Ganesha Purana

15. WHY DURVA GRASS IS OFFERED TO GANESHA

Oh, what fun it was for Analasura, scorching everything down with his fiery vision. His eyes literally emitted fire. Yes, flames of fire! Simply by his look, a person could be charred to death. And he was doing just that. Like a child with a new toy, he was enjoying the deathly game. He sometimes turned his gaze towards heaven to ignite demigods.

After he was sufficiently amused, he would turn towards earth to light up humans. Their shock and terror at the sudden explosion of fire was delightful and satisfying to the perverted demon. It gave him a sense of being the controller of life and death, akin to God himself. Wasn't that the reason he had asked for this boon? He had always yearned for a unique kind of power which would scare people. He wasn't satisfied simply with physical strength or deathlessness. That was no fun. It also involved a lot of effort. The best thing would be to just look at something or someone to create destruction. Many might call him lazy. Yes, he agreed he was lazy. Why lift a finger if lifting the eye was enough?

He felt grateful to Lord Shiva for helping him achieve his dream ambition. He had heard that Shiva was very benevolent and never turned down a request. So, he did some minimal austerities required to please him and . . . wham! Shiva had appeared before him, more than ready to grant him a boon. He promptly asked to be given the ability to generate fire from his eyes. Shiva was amused; nonetheless, he obliged, and his lifelong dream had materialised in a jiffy. From then on, life was a cakewalk. He only had to look at anyone who annoyed him and that was the end of that unfortunate being.

While Analasura was enjoying his new-found powers, his potential victims were in paranoia. How long could they survive or avoid Analasura from gazing at them? Death was certain, sooner or later. And if the boon was granted by Lord Shiva himself, what hope did they have of being saved by anyone? None whatsoever.

Analasura had his sights pinned on the throne of Indra. Afraid, all the gods abandoned heaven and scattered in other planets hiding themselves. Indra too was ill-equipped to deal with this calamity called Analasura. He escaped with the other heavenly residents. Facing many a difficulty after being driven away from their homes, they decided to approach the one person who could still help them. And that was little Ganesha. He was the son of Lord Shiva and as dynamic. His quick wit was always a great resource in getting them out of many a hot soup. And this was one such time.

Ganesha, who had already heard about the antics of Analasura, totally sympathised with the devatas. No way could this go on. The devatas felt a burden being lifted off their chest. With Ganesha on their side, they could win any battle.

"Somehow, I shall put an end to this demon," he promised them all, "please be assured."

Ganesha then mounted his mouse and left for mission impossible. Analasura laughed at all those who came to fight him. He laughed even harder at Ganesha because he had appeared in front of him as a tiny insignificant boy.

"What can you possibly do to me?" he mocked, as his eyes sizzled and threw fireballs at him. Little Ganesha could easily dodge all the fireballs hurled at him.

"Don't waste my time! Show me what you can do," challenged Ganesha.

This angered the demon and he inched closer to him and when his fireballs missed the target, he decided to do the next best thing—swallow him. Swallowing the little boy whole would be easier than burning him down. Further, his tender bones would nourish him too. He smacked his lips as he grabbed Ganesha menacingly. But to his shock, Ganesha caught hold of him and in a complete reversal of situation, swallowed the demon. There was nothing that wouldn't fit in Ganesha's stomach. Including a demon. That done, he burped. Mission accomplished.

Cheers went up all around as the devatas realised what had happened. Ganesha had swallowed Analasura alive! As they cheered and celebrated, Ganesha smiled weakly. He was not feeling comfortable. He grimaced and then he moaned. It was getting worse. An intense heat enveloped him around his stomach and fire was spreading to all parts of his body. Inside his stomach, Analasura was continuing to ooze lethal fire. Soon, Ganesha was writhing from the scorching temperature inside his body. He jumped into a pond nearby but to no effect. The heat continued unabated.

The devatas were startled to see Ganesha in discomfort. They brought sandalwood and applied the paste on his body. Sandalwood could surely cure any heat effect. But Ganesha was still in agony. Indra then asked the moon Chandra to sit on his head with his cooling rays. Chandra obliged. Ganesha looked awfully cute with the moon hanging over his head. The mesmerised demigods spontaneously called him Balchandra. But the moon was also unsuccessful in making any impact on the fire burning inside Ganesha.

News spread that Ganesha was in agony. Lord Shiva arrived and put his snakes around him. No effect. Vishnu came and tied his lotus to him. No effect. Brahma came and offered his daughters Riddhi and Siddhi. No effect.

This was getting alarming. Next, they saw thousands of sages coming towards them. They all had a bunch of *Durva* grass in their hands. A flicker of hope awakened in every sinking heart. Maybe the sages knew something they didn't. After all, sages have knowledge from the Vedas. And sure enough, as soon as they put Durva grass on their patient's head, Ganesha calmed down. As if by miracle, his distress vanished as if it was never there. Everyone finally heaved a sigh of relief. They could finally celebrate the end of Analasura.

An ecstatic Ganesha thanked the sages for their timely help. After that he proclaimed, "Durva grass is really special to me. This simple grass succeeded where even devatas failed. Whoever offers me this grass in devotion will also become special to me. Offering this grass to me is as good as doing pilgrimage and charity."

Thus, more important than flowers, is offering Durva grass to Ganesha. It immediately gives him a sense of gratitude and peace which he spreads in the world.

Source – Ganesha Purana

16.
THE STORY OF TALAKAVERI

It was the event of a lifetime. The wedding of Lord Shiva and Parvati. The who's who of the heavenly, earthly, and hellish planets had all arrived to witness the majestic ceremony. How could anyone miss it? Lord Shiva was everyone's beloved and all were invited to come and bless the divine couple. The crowd of guests comprising gods, rishis, kings, and queens kept swelling and it appeared as if the entire universe had arrived.

And sure enough, the weight on the northern side became unbearable causing the entire universe to plunge and tilt to one side. An alarmed Lord Shiva had to do something quickly to balance it again. He remembered Sage Agastya. Only he had the power to do what Lord Shiva had in mind.

Sage Agastya had performed many miraculous deeds in the past. He was considered the father of healing. He was also the progenitor of *Aditya Hridayam*, hymns to Surya which Lord Rama chanted before his battle with Ravana. He had also written *Naadi Shastra*, a book on astrology. Shiva quickly sought him out and instructed him to leave for the south immediately. Once there, he had to release river Kaveri that he would carry with him in his *kamandalu*. He also instructed Kaveri to flow as per the direction shown by the sage.

Sage Agastya had arrived from a long distance to see Lord Shiva's wedding and was reluctant to leave. He was eager to attend the grand ceremonies. How could he now miss that? Shiva understood Agastya muni's reluctance and assured him that even from the far south, the sage would be able to see the marriage proceedings. A relieved sage Agastya then agreed, and Shiva released the sacred waters of Kaveri from his matted hair into the sage's copper kamandalu with the instruction to let it flow in the south.

Meanwhile, Indra was also in the south, hiding from a powerful demon, Surapaduman, who was harassing Indra. Indra was praying to Lord Shiva to help him out of this sticky situation. He had created a beautiful garden which he would offer to Lord Shiva. But Lord Varuna too was so scared of the demon that he had stopped sending rains for Lord Indra to make his flower offerings. Now Indra was in a fix. How was he to continue his worship without any flowers? As he was thinking about his problems, Narada muni arrived with the solution. He informed Indra that Sage Agastya had left from Kailash with river Kaveri in his kamandalu. Once he arrived, he could somehow get him to allow Kaveri to flow where Indra was located.

Indra then invoked Lord Ganesha to help him. He needed divine help to get Kaveri to flow near him. Sure enough, Ganesha appeared to help the distressed king of heaven. Sage Agastya had reached Podighai mountain range (in Coorg) and was visiting various Shiva *sthalams*. When he reached near where Indra was, Ganesha took the form of a crow. He waited when the sage was meditating and at the right opportunity, he sat on his kamandalu. The alert sage immediately noticed the crow and tried to shoo it away. As soon as the sage raised his hand in the direction of the crow, Kaveri thought it was an indication for her to flow in that direction. Her waters gushed out in all glory taking the sage by surprise.

The crow then turned into a boy and started running away from the sage. Agastya muni suspected some foul play and chased the boy. He so wanted to catch that boy and punish him for his misdeed. Soon the boy transformed into his original form, Ganesha. When the sage realised it was not an ordinary boy but Lord Ganesha, he was very embarrassed and ashamed. He wanted to hit himself for the thought of hitting Ganesha. But Ganesha stopped him and declared that worshipping him here would bestow the seeker with intelligence and wisdom. And the place from where Kaveri began her flow is known as Talakaveri (in Karnataka) located in the Brahmagiri hill near Bhagamandala, which is one of the seven sacred rivers of Sapta Sindhus in the Hindu scriptures. Mother Kaveri is part of Ganga and is also referred to as Dakshina Ganga.

Source – Shiva Purana

17.
THE BENEVOLENCE OF GANESHA ON GANESH CHATURTHI

Ganesha happily looked down from his heavenly abode to see the exciting festivities happening on earth. It was Ganesha Chaturthi, a season Ganesha loved. He got invitations from so many places, and he felt supremely pampered. He peered through the clouds, to see the busy scenes as his vision zoomed into one village in India. It was a beehive of activities as every home in that village was preparing for his arrival. The women were most busy with cooking, cleaning, decorating, dressing, and so many other things. The fragrance of jaggery-laden modaks wafted through the air all the way to heaven. Children in new clothes peeped into kitchens to lay their hands on something delicious before they were seen and sent packing. The warm glow radiating all the way from earth was truly comforting.

Suddenly, a thought struck him. How about going down himself to be amongst those people on earth. Wouldn't that be more of an enjoyable experience? Celebrating in the midst of his followers would be so much better than sitting here alone and squinting through the clouds. So many obstacles blocked his path of vision. Sometimes a slow-moving planet would station itself between him and earth, spoiling the live streaming. Yes, it would be a treat for him to spend time there in person.

He quickly disguised himself and descended into the quaint village that seemed to have a huge fan following of Ganesha. His prankster mind was already busy at work, thinking of how he would trick the villagers by not revealing his identity. He would roam about freely without being discovered.

A dirty, unkempt boy entered the village. Although he looked emaciated, he had a big belly. His big ears stood out as did his small eyes. Holding a fistful of rice and a spoonful of milk, he marched towards one of the houses and knocked on the door.

"Excuse me, can you please prepare some rice pudding for me, using this rice and milk?" he asked the lady of the house.

The lady was clearly annoyed at her busy routine being interrupted. She looked at him from top to bottom, crinkled her nose and said, "Do I look like your servant? Don't even enter my house, you unclean boy."

Disappointed, the boy turned around and looked for another house. Surely someone would cook rice pudding for him. Ganesha devotees were known to be kind-hearted. Sure of finding success at the next house, he knocked another door. But frankly, no one had time for a boy who looked like a beggar and that too someone who wanted them to make rice pudding with his ingredients. Wherever he went, he was shooed away unceremoniously.

A young girl refused because she couldn't cook the minute quantity of rice. Another woman had more important things to do to please her Ganesha. Another said she did not entertain beggars and he was too dirty to enter her clean house. And in the last house he was returning from, the lady actually accused him of contaminating her pure house. The little boy was dejected. He had not asked for much. Just for a simple rice pudding. He had shown his fistful of rice and spoonful of milk to so many people. Addressing them as *dada, chacha, mata, mausi*, but none had obliged. Was there no one who would cook for him?

What was wrong with the people here? Were they so immersed in celebrating Ganesha Chaturthi that they were unwilling to feed a hungry child?

Lost in his thoughts, he stumbled into a poverty-stricken courtyard which looked like it had been neglected for months. No one had even bothered to sweep the area; heaps of dried leaves and branches lay scattered here and there. A bucket near the well gave testimony to some human presence inside the hut. The little boy's hopes soared. He could still find someone to cook for him.

He went towards the dilapidated hut as quickly as his legs could carry him, excited to find out what was waiting for him. Disappointment or rice pudding? He yelled at the door, "Is anyone home?" When there was no reply, he hesitantly took a step inside.

In the darkness, he could see the silhouette of a frail old woman sleeping on the floor. She was too old to cook probably. Yet, he had to ask. He went closer and touched her. The old grandmother opened her eyes. Her kind eyes locked into his and she smiled kindly. Encouraged, the boy said, "Grandmother, I have this with me," he showed her his possessions, "can you cook rice pudding for me?"

"Son, this is way too little. It will get burnt immediately the minute I put it on fire. Besides, I have no pots to cook it in."

"Grandmother, go and borrow a large pot. Just do as I say," urged the poor boy, his eyes gleaming with hope.

The frail old lady knew there could be no pudding with the meagre quantities of rice and milk. Nonetheless, she humoured him and went and borrowed a large pot. The boy danced when he saw the pot. Hurriedly he poured the rice and milk into the pot. When grandmother looked inside the pot, it was full to the brim. Shocked, she let out an incredulous gasp and turned to look at him. "How did the pot get filled?" she asked. The boy smiled and winked.

"Grandmother, you please make the pudding while I take a bath in the river and come back." The boy dashed out excited at the turn of events.

The old lady turned her attention to the pot and busied herself in making the special rice pudding, all the time thinking about the magical way in which the pot had filled. Everything about the pudding was magical, including the delicious aroma entering her nostrils. The creamy thick *kheer* in the pot was the most appetising thing she had seen in her long life. It was so tempting that suddenly, waiting for the little boy to return was unbearable. She had to eat the pudding now. She quickly transferred some of it on a plate and first offered it to the Lord Ganesha deity in her house. Next, she took a plate for herself and gobbled down chunks of it with her hand. Only when she was done did she breathe again. So mesmerised was she with the fragrance, appearance, and the taste of the dessert. But now that she had had her fill, she was hit by pangs of guilt. How insensitive of her not to wait for the boy.

Soon the boy returned. A plate of rice pudding was waiting for him.

"Where's your plate?" he asked.

"I couldn't wait to eat. I'm sorry I had some before you came back. But I will sit with you as you eat," said the embarrassed grandmother. The boy pushed his plate aside and said, "I'm not hungry either."

"What happened?" the grandmother asked with concern, "are you alright?"

Something was not right, and the old lady knew from all her life experiences that this boy was not ordinary.

"Tell me, who are you? From your hands you poured a pot full of milk and rice. I ate four bowls of it and yet the pot is full. And now you don't want to eat also," she admonished him, trying to scare him into telling the truth.

"Grandmother, you already fed me when you offered the plate to Ganesha."

So saying, the little boy leapt up and transformed himself into Ganesha.

"The entire village is preparing to welcome me but when I came, no one had time for me. Only you showed kindness and cooked for me. When you offered it, I had a hearty meal. Thank you for your hospitality. Now ask me for any boon and it shall be granted."

The old lady had tears in her eyes. She, of all people, had received Ganesha's causeless mercy. She thanked her lucky stars and asked Ganesha to give her a life full of devotion that was free from obstacles.

Ganesha bestowed on her devotion along with unlimited wealth.

Source – Folk Tales

18.
HOW GANESHA BECAME VEDVYASA'S SCRIBE TO WRITE THE MAHABHARATA

Did you know that Vedvyasa, the author of the greatest true story *Mahabharata*, was the grandfather of the Pandavas and the Kauravas? Moreover, he had such a long life that he lived even after his grandchildren left the world. There are more interesting facts behind the writing of the *Mahabharata* that will amaze you.

Vedvyasa was deep in meditation in his ashram nestled amongst snow-clad Himalayan peaks. Since many days he had been thinking about writing the *Mahabharata*. But somehow, he wasn't mentally ready for it. Even as he meditated, his thoughts were centred on when he would actually get down to writing it. But what he had not realised was that he was not the only one thinking about it. The creator of the universe Brahmaji was also eager for Vedvyasa to begin the work. Wanting to inspire him, Brahma decided to pay Vedvyasa a surprise visit.

Vedvyasa was startled to see Brahmaji. Brahmaji explained to him why he was the best person to write this epic volume. "Have you not witnessed the entire event live? Are you not intimately familiar with each and every character of the *Mahabharata*?" Brahmaji demanded to know from Vedvyasa as he saw his hesitation.

Vedvyasa contemplated and presented his case, "It would help if someone could write it for me as I dictate."

"Ask the intelligent Ganesha to help you," suggested Brahma as he vanished from the ashram.

Vedvyasa took the suggestion seriously and meditated on Lord Ganesha. Lord Ganesha now made an appearance. Vedvyasa asked him if he would write for him. Besides being intelligent, Ganesha was naughty too. He said, "But I have a condition!"

A condition? Vedvyasa was startled.

"I write fast, and I write non-stop," said Ganesha playfully, "so if you break in between then I will not continue after that."

Vedvyasa was thinking fast. Not that he needed breaks, but he did not want any kind of pressure. He smiled at Ganesha and said, "I have a condition too!"

Now it was Ganesha's turn to be startled. He hadn't expected that. He waited eagerly to hear the condition.

"I appreciate your dedication," said Vedvyasa lovingly, "but my condition is that you will write what I speak only after you have understood the meaning. Please do not write mechanically."

Ganesha accepted the condition sportingly. And the two began the historical process of putting the *Mahabharata* in writing. But whenever the shrewd Vedvyasa needed a moment to compose a verse, he would throw a puzzling verse at Ganesha to keep him pondering over it. As per the condition, Ganesha would take time to understand the import of the verse and only then write. This would give Vedvyasa enough time to compose further verses.

This explains the presence of many puzzling verses in the epic. In fact, the *Mahabharata* contains 8800 such complicated verses that are called *kuta* shlokas.

We can attempt to grasp one such shloka –

nadījalaṁ keśava nāri ketur
nagāhvayo nāma nag.risūnu.
eṣo 'ngana veṣa dharaḥ kirīṭī
jitvā vayaṁ neṣyati cādya gāvaḥ
(*Mahabharata*, Virata parva 39.10)

Nadī means river; jalaṁ means water; keśava is the name of a person but what is their connection? Nāri means woman; ketur means flag, so what relation do they hold? What does nagarishnu, son of bugle mean? The literal meaning seems ambiguous. However, when seen from a deeper perspective, it makes a lot of sense.

Read differently and the shloka unearths the right meaning –

nadīja lankeśa vana ari ketur
nagāhvayo nāma nag.risūnu.

eṣo 'nganā veṣa dharaḥ kirīṭī
jitva avayaṁ neṣyati cādya gāvaḥ
(*Mahabharata*, Virata parva 39.10)

nadīja - Bhishma, the son of Ganga; lankeśa - Ravana; vana - forest; ari - enemy; ketu - flag; nagāhvayo - Arjuna who has the name of arjuna tree, or Arjuna who is the son of Indra, who was the enemy of the flying mountain; anganā veṣa - in the form of woman; kirīṭī - Arjuna; jitva - to win; ava - to protect; yam - he; neṣyati - not to take; gāvaḥ - cows.

Translation – O son of Ganga (Bhishma)! Hanuman, who burnt the forest of Lankesha Ravana, is sitting on the flag of Arjuna, the son of Indra, who has now appeared in the guise of a woman and come to take away the cows; please protect us from him. (Drona said this to Bhishma)

When he would come across such complicated verses, Ganesha would take his time to first decipher them, understand them, and only then write them. As the writing of the *Mahabharata* continued, something interesting happened in between. Ganesha's feather, which he used for writing, broke. It was too much writing for the delicate feather to handle. But

Ganesha had a commitment, and he could not stop writing. A promise was a promise after all. He then pulled out his own tusk and used that for writing. And that explains why Ganesha has one tusk! In most pictures, Ganesha is seen with one tusk while he holds the other tusk in his hand.

Source – Ganesha Purana

19.
THE SLAYING OF TRIPURASURA

Shiva was flabbergasted. Never had he ever experienced anything like this before! Never had he faced any kind of obstacle in any mission. He had attacked and successfully slayed innumerable demons, but this was the first time he had run into trouble. He couldn't understand why his chariot wheel was stuck. Not just stuck, but the entire chariot seemed to be on the verge of collapse. It was as if he was using an old and rusted chariot which had seen better days. But Shiva knew that was definitely not the case. His chariot had never malfunctioned. Somehow, with herculean effort, he and his army managed to reach Tripura to fight the so-called invincible demon Tripurasura. "Now it will be easy," thought Shiva. But how mistaken he was. One calamity followed another and there was no end to it.

When Shiva's army of gods saw the size of the demon army, they were terrified by the sheer number. They would never be able to defeat a humungous army and that too, not an ordinary army but an army full of world class demons. They could hear the thunderous laugh of Tripurasura challenging them to march forward. Overcome with weakness and their heads feeling dizzy, they fled from the battlefield leaving a lone Shiva behind. Facing defeat, Shiva too made himself invisible and disappeared from there.

Back home, he tried to figure out what had gone wrong. He had a feeling that his son Ganesha was somehow involved in all of this. Wasn't it Ganesha who blessed Tripurasura with the boon? Shiva's mouth distorted and his body trembled thinking of how cunning Tripurasura had been and how much he had already suffered because of him.

Born from the sneeze of Sage Gritsamada in Treta yuga, Tripurasura had shown wicked qualities right from his childhood. Unlike his father who was very devoted to Ganesha, this boy had been ruthlessly ambitious wanting to rule the three worlds. However hard his father tried to instil devotion in him, he remained adamant and as stubborn as a dog's tail. Since his father had taught him many mantras that could please Ganesha, his manipulative mind cooked up a sizzling scheme to realise his ambition.

He chanted the Ganesha mantra to please Lord Ganesha for 5000 years. Seeing his fierce determination for chanting, Ganesha was highly impressed and appeared before him. Naturally, he wanted to bless him with a boon.

No prizes for guessing what he wanted. "I want to rule all the three worlds."

And because demons are very attached to their material bodies, they want power for eternity. So, he also added, "Please also bless me that no god, no divine power, and no human can ever defeat me."

And he stood there with folded hands in false humility.

"So shall it be," said Ganesha, "however, only Lord Shiva will have the power to defeat you. Moreover, I give you three cities. As long as you live in these cities, you will be undefeatable. But if

Lord Shiva so desires, he can overpower you with his arrows."

That was enough power for the demon who immediately declared himself Tripurasura, conqueror of three worlds. He went on a battle spree, driving away humans from earth, Indra from heaven, Brahma from Brahmaloka, and Vishnu from Vaikuntha.

The homeless gods found shelter in the Himalayas. Lord Shiva and Parvati too relocated to the Mandar Mountain. The atmosphere was tense. Homeless and helpless, no one knew how to fight back.

As Shiva was reminiscing about past events and trying to find a hidden clue as to what had gone wrong and why had he faced so many obstacles, he was pleasantly surprised by the arrival of a visitor. It was always a pleasure to talk to Narada muni. He was a bottomless box of wisdom and when in the mood, gave priceless advice.

Shiva opened his heart and soul to Narada muni to find the mystery behind his defeat. He revealed how his chariot fell apart stopping him in his tracks and how his army turned to jelly, simply unable to fight the demons. All this was a new phenomenon, never encountered before. Did it have something to do with Ganesha, Shiva asked the wise sage.

Narada muni closed his eyes. He needed to meditate on all the information so he could process it. When he opened his eyes, his face lit up. The smile on his face indicated he had found the answer. Shiva found hope returning to him.

"Lord Shiva, there is a very simple connection to everything you have experienced and yes, you are right, it is all connected to Ganesha."

Lord Shiva beamed. His intuition had never let him down. He eagerly waited to hear Narada muni's nectarean words.

"It was your instruction and blessing to Ganesha that if one remembered him before embarking on any important task, he would surely find success. Forgetfulness of Ganesha would result in failure. So, you and your army, in a hurry to reach Tripurasura, forgot to remember him and seek his auspiciousness. This was all the more important because it was Ganesha who bestowed the boon to the demon, and it was Ganesha who put in the clause that only you could defeat him."

Shiva became grave when he heard this. It was true that remembering Ganesha removed all difficulties from one's path. It was also true that he had not followed the protocol.

He looked at Narada muni, desperately hoping to hear a solution from him.

Narada did not disappoint him. "It is never too late. You can invoke auspiciousness from Ganesha even now and then proceed to attack Tripurasura. You will not fail again."

Having done his job, the great devotee of Vishnu disappeared as quickly as he had appeared, leaving behind the echo of his chant, "Narayana, Narayana."

Shiva quickly prepared himself to invoke the power of Ganesha. After chanting the recommended mantras, Lord Ganesha was pleased and sanctioned the success of Lord Shiva's mission. A confident Lord Shiva then attacked and destroyed the three cities with his bow and lost no time in liberating Tripurasura. The gods sighed in relief as law and order was restored once again and life for all living entities limped back to normalcy.

Source - Shiva Purana

20.
WHY GANESHA HAS VERMILLION ON HIS HEAD

Demons always have a one-track agenda. To be invincible and supremely powerful. Sindurasura is the perfect example of this. His mind worked in such creative ways to achieve his one ambition—rule over the gods.

Sindurasura, like his name suggested, was deep vermilion in colour, easily distinguishable from even far away. No one had any difficulty in recognising him. In fact, when he walked through a forest, it appeared as if the forest was on fire. His appearance was so fiery and scary that no one dared venture near him. So, he was a little surprised when he sensed a presence nearby one day when he was strolling in a forest. Smelling his way towards the living entity, he found himself face to face with Lord Brahma sitting in meditation.

Now demons have been known to perform austerities for thousands of years simply to get a darshan of Lord Brahma. Hiranyakasipu had spent thousands of years in penance to get a boon from him. And here he was, getting darshan without any effort. Sindurasura couldn't help but rub his hands in glee. This was too good an opportunity to let go of. Here was a God-given chance to become immortal staring him in the eye. To become the most powerful demon ever. His mind went into overdrive to take advantage of this surreal situation. Bang! Within minutes he hit upon a devilish plan to con Brahma into giving away what he wanted.

Getting into action, he reduced his size to minuscule proportions. He became so tiny that he entered into Lord Brahma's nostril and made himself comfortable in the nasal cavity. He waited patiently for Brahma to come out of his samadhi. The wait was endless. Because time in heaven is non-existent. The normally impatient demon became patience personified because he knew the end of the wait would be very sweet for him. After what seemed like an eternity, Brahma finally stirred. The movement of his body was an indication that he was emerging out of meditation. As soon as Sindurasura was sure that Brahma was in his external senses, he began to irritate the nostril.

Brahma, surprised with the irritation in his nose, rubbed his nose. But the irritation increased and reflexively, he sneezed. That was the plan! To get Brahma to sneeze. And with the sneeze, Sindurasura was ejected forcefully out of Brahma's nose. Brahma saw something red shooting out. He was surprised. Sindurasura landed on his palm.

"I am your son," he said, "born from your sneeze."

That was the trick! He tricked Brahma into believing that he was born from him.

Immediately, Brahma relaxed. He caressed Sindurasura as a wave of paternal love surged within him.

"My son!"

Sindurasura beamed at the success of his sinister plan. It didn't take too much to convince him! Now

Brahma was putty in his hands, and he could mould him in any way he wanted.

"Father, I'm your son," said he, tugging at the strings of Brahma's heart.

A son is special, and I will give him a boon, thought the innocent Brahma. Considering his small size, Brahma said, "My son, you are so tiny; so, I bless you that no one will ever be able to defeat you with any kind of weapon. Your powers will always protect you and keep you safe. Additionally, whoever you touch will turn into ashes. You will have nothing to fear."

Wow! This is too good to be true, thought Sindurasura.

Brahma had something more to say. "But remember, your powers will not work against Ganesha. He is the only one who is immune to your touch."

Sindurasura was hardly listening. He didn't care about what Brahma had to say now. He quickly turned into his normal demonic size and laughed at the naïve Brahma.

"Oh Lord Brahma, I am Sindurasura, a demon. Not your son as you believed me to be. But too bad! Now I have your blessings. I shall do as I please."

Delirious with joy, Sindurasura went berserk. He did not know how to contain his excitement. He hardly knew what he was doing or saying.

"I want to test my powers. And since no one else is here, I will touch you and see if you burn into ashes."

Now Lord Brahma was in trouble. A boon given by him was being tried out against him. Of course, it would work and if Sindurasura touched him, he would be reduced to ashes.

Before the demon could move, Brahma made a run for his life. Never had this ever happened before where the recipient of the boon had turned against him. Thinking fast, he ran towards Kailash. Perhaps Lord Shiva would know how to handle the situation. In fact, he should know because he was the lord of all demons. Finding hope in that thought, Brahma quickened his pace to reach Kailash, constantly keeping an eye on Sindurasura to maintain a safe distance between them.

He barged inside the gates of Kailash Parbat, without waiting for permission. Close at his heels, Sindurasura too followed him inside. Who would dare to stop him now? Puffed with pride about his newfound power, he entered the sacred precincts of Kailash without any hesitation. Even the demigods were hiding behind dark clouds to avoid bumping into him. Exerting his power gave him a special kind of kick now. No matter where Brahma ran, nothing could save him. He imagined the world at his feet and how he would rule over everyone. At regular intervals, he smiled, laughed, or simply smirked. He was the lord of lords, and everyone had better know it.

Brahma had reached the inner chamber of Shiva. Parvati was seated beside him. As soon as Sindurasura's eyes fell on the divine beauty of Parvati, he fell head over heels in love with her. He completely forgot what he was supposed to do and instead approached Parvati lustily.

"O beautiful goddess, please be mine." He extended his hand to her.

The problem with demons is that they have no intelligence as such. He made two stupid mistakes. He ignored Brahma when he told him that his powers would be rendered useless against Ganesha. A wise person always pays heed to the weak spots. And now he was trying to lure the goddess into an alliance with him in front of her husband and son. Yes, Ganesha was standing behind his mother. As soon as he made an attempt to hold her hand, Ganesha stopped him and struck him so hard that he exploded into pieces. A shower of vermilion pieces scattered all over with a few falling on Ganesha. Parvati hugged her brave son and decorated the vermilion piece on his forehead as a reminder of his feat. Till today, Ganesha sports vermilion (*kum kum*) on his forehead to remind all demons—beware of Ganesha.

Source – Ganesha Purana

21.
HOW THE EIGHTH JYOTIRLING TRYAMBAKA WAS ESTABLISHED

Long, long ago, there was a severe drought in the land of Bharata. So severe that it had not rained for a hundred years. A hundred years without any rainfall is a long time indeed. Whenever calamities befall mankind, it's natural to ask for help from the higher powers. This has been the tradition since time immemorial. It thus fell on the shoulders of Sage Gautama and his wife Ahalya to appease Varuna, the lord of oceans and water. They had already been in meditation for ten thousand years when they realised that the earth was affected by a lack of water for the last hundred years.

From Brahmaparvata, their mountain abode, they began their prayers to Varuna, to save mankind from sure death.

Pleased by the purity of Sage Gautama, Varuna appeared before him. It was a pleasure for Varuna to serve sages like Gautama rishi, who lived their lives solely for the benefit of man.

"Please let it rain," pleaded Gautama to Varuna.

"Ask me anything else," said an apologetic Varuna, "for this is not within my jurisdiction."

The intelligent sage knew Varuna was right, so he immediately changed his request.

"Then please give me a spring in the forest near my ashram which is perennial. Which will never dry no matter what."

"Yes, I grant you this boon," replied Varuna who was relieved to fulfil at least the small wish of a big mahatma. He admired rishi Gautama's intelligence and left soon after.

Gautama rishi, being saintly, allowed everyone to use that spring freely. Of course, his disciples used it knowing well that the spring was a result of years of their guru's and his wife's penance and austerities. However, the rishis from the surrounding mountains and forests eagerly came there too without acknowledging the role of the great sage. No matter, because it did not perturb the sage one bit. It was a perennial source that had sprung up to benefit all.

Alas, not all sages can show the same mettle. They forgot that the life-giving spring was the fruit of Gautama rishi's love for them after millennia of hardships. Their wives gradually began to think of the spring as exclusively theirs and prevented even Gautama rishi's disciples from drawing water from it.

Rather than the indignity of fighting, the disciples chose to withdraw. When news reached Ahalya, she herself began to go to fetch water to maintain peace in their quiet dwellings. This had an adverse effect on her health. Physically, it was too taxing to carry buckets and buckets of water over and above her life of austerity and ashram duties. Mentally, the wives of the sages harassed her by preventing her from going near the spring. Taking all of this in her stride, she still continued with her duties just so that there could be peaceful co-existence.

But strange are the ways of human nature. These vile women complained to their husbands about Ahalya harassing them. Concocting their own facts which were figments of their imagination, they poisoned the minds of their husbands. They painted a dark picture portraying the sage and his wife as wicked and sinful. Believing their wives' words to be true, the sages got into action. Sadly, they did not verify the truth. They did not even stop to think how Ahalya, a most pious lady, wife of the sage Gautama, could stoop so low. Somehow, we are always ready to believe the worst in others, ignoring the worst within us.

They sat in meditation, minds focused on Lord Ganesha. They wanted his help in teaching their enemy a lesson. All they wanted was the sagely couple out of their hermitage and out of the forest so that they could do as they pleased. Ganesha appeared on their request. But he was extremely hurt on hearing why they had called him.

"Lord, please help us in driving away Gautama muni from his ashram. We do not want him nearby."

Shocked to the core, Ganesha was speechless. His mind was racing trying to figure out how to handle these sages who had come with the request of harming someone. That too, not an ordinary mortal but the great sage Gautama. Hurting exalted sages was a sure shot way of falling off from the spiritual path.

It was a sensitive matter for Ganesha. He had to deal with his own followers in a way that they would come to their senses and also punish them for their evil deeds.

He turned himself into a weak and old cow and placed himself in Gautama muni's field. It appeared as if the cow was eating everything in the field and destroying the crop. When Gautama saw the cow, he looked around for his disciples. Finding himself alone, he himself went to drive the cow away from the field.

Using a blade of grass, he touched the cow. A blade of grass can under no circumstance qualify as a weapon. But since that cow was not a cow and Ganesha in disguise, he acted as if hurt and feigned death. He collapsed then and there, causing Gautama to think he had killed a cow. Alarmed and disturbed, Gautama couldn't believe what had just happened. By mere touch of grass, the cow had died. Learned in scriptures, he knew killing the cow was a grave sin. Soon, the other sages gathered. It was just the opportunity they needed to ask Gautama to leave for committing a heinous sin such as this.

Ashamed and embarrassed, Gautama left with his wife. He would do further austerities to atone himself from this sin. The sages had suggested they circumambulate the Brahmaparvata a hundred times and purify themselves by bathing in a hundred sacred waters. The sagely couple readily complied. They also prayed to Lord Shiva to solve the water shortage for the benefit of all. If Ganga could flow from his head to the ashram, it would solve so many problems. Lord Shiva was happy to execute the sage's desire. Everyone loves a kind saint who desires the welfare of others more than their own.

Shiva released the sacred Ganga from his head, and she cascaded down to Gautama muni's ashram. But this was not what Ganga wanted to do. She did not want to leave Kailash or Lord Shiva, so she requested him along with Parvati to stay with her. Thus, the eighth Jyotirling Tryambaka was established. On the way, she would have drowned and destroyed all the other ashrams in the vicinity including those who had harassed the compassionate sage and Ahalya. But Gautama asked Ganga to forgive them all. The sages performed the same austerities that they had asked Gautama to do and asked for his forgiveness.

Thus, Lord Ganesha did not disappoint the sages in any way and yet helped them see their mistake. All's well that ends well.

Source – Brahma Purana

22.
THE CONQUEST OF GAJASURA

Parvati had searched high and low, but she could not find him. Where could he be, she wondered. Last when she had seen her husband, Lord Shiva was deep in meditation in his favourite asana. And the next thing she knew was that he had disappeared. She's seen Shiva do many strange things before and it did not surprise her any more. But never had he disappeared without a trace. After a thorough search of Kailash, she spent a day in restless anxiety waiting for him to return. Perhaps he had to leave for an emergency. She consoled herself. But when a full day elapsed and he was still missing, she realised something serious was going on. She needed help to find him.

The only person she could think of was Vishnu. She approached him frantically, "O' Lord Vishnu, Lord Shiva has not been home since yesterday. I don't even know where he is. Can You help me find him?" she pleaded helplessly.

Vishnu pondered over her words for a minute and then replied, "Dear Parvati, Lord Shiva is too innocent for his own good. I am sure he has landed himself in some trouble with a demon. He is prone to do that. He is not called Bholenath or Ashutosh for nothing."

Vishnu's confident smile gave Parvati some hope.

"I will find him," He reassured her.

After Parvati left, Vishnu used His meditative powers to locate the whereabouts of Shiva. What He learnt left Him stunned. How many unique ways could demons find to capture Shiva? He was simply amazed with His latest finding. A demon called Gajasura (an elephant demon) had done austerities to please Shiva. The compassionate Shiva was pleased and sanctioned a boon. The demon asked Shiva to stay in his stomach. Shiva agreed and entered his stomach. That was it. Shiva was now inside Gajasura's stomach oblivious to all the mayhem outside because of his disappearance.

How does one bring back someone from inside a stomach? That was the dilemma Vishnu had to solve now. He could possibly use the same methodology that the demon had used. Vishnu allowed Himself half a smile as a plan along those lines began to take shape in His mind.

He went to Kailash to speak to Nandi bull, Shiva's faithful follower. Nandi was equally concerned about his lord's disappearing act and was trying to console Parvati. Vishnu outlined His plan to Nandi, and he readily agreed. The two of them departed for Gajasura's demonic abode to implement their plan.

They presented themselves in front of the demon as entertainment artists. Vishnu played a melodious flute while a well-decorated Nandi danced to His tune. The couple looked so much in sync and their movements were so graceful and heart-warming that it pleased Gajasura immensely. The charming couple had stolen his heart so much so that he granted them a gift in sheer bliss.

"Ask for anything your heart desires and it shall be yours!"

He said this more out of ignorant pride than anything else. The flutist jumped upon the chance but not before teasing him a bit.

"Are you sure you can give me anything my heart desires? What if you can't?"

The very thought of being challenged was unbearable for Gajasura. "Of course, I can give you anything. I have all the powers," Gajasura asserted while he thought of Shiva inside his stomach as he said this. Who in the world could boast of imprisoning Shiva inside his body?

"Then I desire that you release Lord Shiva from your stomach and let him go back to Kailash," said the flutist capitalising on the demon's pride.

Taken aback by the request, Gajasura wondered who the flutist was.

"How did you know Lord Shiva is inside my stomach? Who are you?" he asked, baffled to the core.

Vishnu revealed His majestic form to the demon. Gajasura had no option but to release his prized prisoner. When Lord Shiva emerged from inside, Gajasura asked forgiveness and expressed his desire.

"If not immortal, at least make sure that I am always remembered in this world. I always want to live in the memories of the world."

Shiva agreed to grant his request and cut off his head. He carried the head back with him to Kailash. At the gates of Kailash, outside his home, he was accosted by a strange boy he had never seen before. Worse, he was actually preventing him from entering his own abode.

"My mother has said no one should be allowed to enter until my father returns." He kept repeating the same words over and over again in spite of Shiva telling him that he was the master of this abode. Impatient to go inside, he cut off the boy's head with his sword. He did not care who his mother or father was. He just wanted to meet Parvati. Parvati too was overjoyed to see him back. His joy paled immediately when Parvati asked him a question.

"Did you see the boy at the gate? He is our son. I created him from dough while you were gone, to help me guard our house. I call him Vinayak."

And Parvati saw the colour draining off Lord Shiva's face.

"What happened? Why are you so pale?"

Shiva could not hide the truth. "I cut off his head because he was not allowing me to enter."

Now Parvati's face turned pale. She nearly fainted. But Shiva was a quick thinker.

"Wait a minute. I will revive him immediately."

He ran towards the boy, carrying Gajasura's head in his hands. He placed the elephant head on the boy and quickly brought him back to life. The boy stood up and ran to his mother. Parvati was so happy to see her son back that she didn't mind that he had an elephant head. He was lovable to her any which way. Shiva then blessed his son that he would be the master of all his followers (Ganesha) and the most loved god in the world. In this way, he also fulfilled Gajasura's desire to be remembered forever. He would always be remembered as Ganesha.

Source – Shiva Purana

23.
THE BIRTH OF LORD GAJANANA

King Varenya's happiness knew no bounds. He hurried to tell his wife the good news. In his haste, he stumbled and fumbled, excited to reach his inner chamber at the earliest. Years had passed without them having a child. Many a times he had wondered if his past karmas were so bad that he would never have the pleasure of holding his own child. Not a day passed without lamenting about the absence of an infant in their lap. But thankfully, that was all in the past. The present was full of excitement. He was bursting at his seams with so much joy, eager to share the ecstatic news first with his wife and then the whole world.

"Pushpika, Pushpika!" he shouted running the entire length of corridors before reaching his inner chambers.

Queen Pushpika heard her husband's voice coming from a distance and her first reaction was of anxiety. What had happened for the king to be screaming like that? But his voice did not sound as if he was in distress. She knew him too well to know that it was something positive rather than negative. She rushed out to meet him halfway. They bumped into each other, and the king hugged his wife as soon as he saw her. After squeezing her hard, he carried her and went round in circles jubilantly laughing.

Finally, he put her down and even though he was out of breath, he whispered, "Our prayers have been answered. Lord Ganesha has promised me that he will appear as our child!" Now it was Queen Pushpika's turn to go mad with joy. She jumped up and down squealing in delight.

Once the excited couple quietened down, they began to plan ahead. Time flew and soon the day arrived when Queen Pushpika delivered a bonny baby. She was exhausted from the process and was resting in her private room. Both mother and child were under heavy security. No one was allowed to go near the baby.

However, demons don't care for security. Word of the queen having given birth to a child had spread. A demon took it as a challenge to kidnap the child and prove his superior powers. Since the palace guards were not expecting any threat from anywhere, they lapsed in their duties. Taking advantage of the security gap, the demon made his way into the nursery. The queen lay asleep in the adjacent room. Without creating any disturbance, the demon picked up the infant and disappeared.

A great commotion ensued when it was discovered the child was missing! The guards were shell-shocked. The king lost his senses. The queen was sleeping so she had no idea of the mayhem around her. No one knew what to do and where to search.

Lord Gajanana, who was born to Lord Shiva and Parvati at the same time, confided to his father that he wanted to go to his devotee's house, King

Varenya. One purpose of his appearance was to please his devotee. Since their child had been kidnapped, Gajanana himself would pose as his child. Lord Shiva instructed Nandi, the divine bull, to carry Gajanana to King Varenya's kingdom and gently place him near the sleeping queen.

"It is imperative that the queen not know about the kidnapped infant and that she considers Gajanana to be her own," was his crisp instruction. Nandi left immediately to carry out his master's wish. He delivered the four-handed, elephant-faced baby near the sleeping mother, Queen Pushpika, and returned to Mount Kailash.

Morning came and the queen rose from her slumber. Fondly, she touched her baby with her eyes closed. The minute she opened her eyes and saw the child, she recoiled in horror. How could any child have an elephant face? How could any baby have four hands? This was an aberration of nature! How would she face the world holding an abnormal child like this? She could not even go near the child, leave alone raise him. Unable to bear the tragedy, she fainted, falling on the floor. Her attendants and maids rushed to help her. But the sight of the abnormal child created panic in them and one by one all of them fainted.

As soon as word reached the king that something strange was going on, he hurried there. He saw a room full of people on the floor and an abnormal, elephant-faced infant happily playing by himself. He quickly understood the sequence of events and called his trusted minister.

"Take this hideous infant away from the palace and leave him in the heart of the jungle. This cannot be a royal child, the heir to my lineage." With a hard heart, he thought disposing off the child was the best option. At once, the soldiers carried away the strange child to abandon him far, far away from the kingdom. They left him near a lake that had crystal clear water, assured that wild animals would soon pounce upon him and make him their meal. They reported to the king that the child had been adequately taken care of. The king hung his head in sorrow at the biggest loss in his life.

Meanwhile, the infant was joyous at the lakeside in the pristine natural environment. Parashar muni frequented that lake every day and the infant grabbed his attention by the sounds he was making.

The muni was surprised to see the oddities in the child. Was it a trap cast by Indra? Afraid that the child could spell disaster for him if it was a trap, the muni remained reluctantly away. But even from far he could decipher some divine markings on the child's feet. Surely, it couldn't be a trap.

He inched towards the baby now fully convinced that it was nothing less than a divine being lying in front of him. Happily, he picked up the child and took him home. His wife was overjoyed and thanked God for the divine gift. Gajanana slowly grew up in Parashar muni's ashram and killed the demon Sindura. When King Varenya heard about Gajanana's heroic acts, he ran to the ashram. In repentance, he worshipped the Lord and begged for forgiveness. By acting in haste, the king had unknowingly banished the Lord from his life.

Source – Ganesha Purana

24.
THE STORY OF GANESHA'S BANANA TREE BRIDE

The wedding procession marched on with great pomp and show. No one wanted to be left out of the grand celebration. After all, it was a mega event, the wedding of Lord Ganesha. Guests flocked from all planets, from Brahma loka to Patal loka, to witness the union. Ganesha himself was excited seeing the huge procession.

Gandharvas, kinnaras, yakshas, ganas, bhutas, pretas . . . were all immersed in joyous festivities. How he loved all the music and dancing! And not to forget the feasting. He chuckled at the thought of *chappan bhoga* or a wide buffet of the choicest foods and sweets waiting for him. How he loved weddings, more so his! He glanced around, drinking in the fluid scene of merrymaking.

All this action was making him hungry. Whatever the occasion, hunger was his constant companion. His trunk searched his pockets for some modaks. Nothing like some delicious golden modaks dipped in jaggery to calm him down. However, his trunk searched all over but couldn't find a single modak. He next shot his trunk into his carry bag. No luck there either. Now Ganesha was in panic mode. How would he survive the journey, the event, the rituals, without modaks by his side? Impossible! He knew he couldn't. He was already pale without his sugar shots. And it would be shameful to faint during his own marriage procession. His body trembled at the thought of him falling unconscious from weakness. He decided to do something about it.

Looking around frantically, he hoped there would be someone who could help him. But everyone seemed much too busy immersed in talking and dancing. There was only one option left for him. He himself would have to go back home and ask mother to pack some laddus. Only she would understand his plight, knowing him in and out.

But what if people noticed his absence? How embarrassing to be caught returning with laddus and modaks. Surely less embarrassing than fainting right there. His mind battled for a few minutes trying to figure out what was less embarrassing. It was a war between etiquette and hunger. Hunger won hands down. In fact, the war barely lasted a few fractions of a second. The winner was a no-brainer.

Satisfied with his decision, Ganesha slowed down trying to make his absence inconspicuous. No one had noticed that Ganesha was missing from his own marriage procession. He wheeled around and scuttled back home. Suddenly, his energy had returned. The thought of successfully stashing up on his modaks gave him an adrenaline rush. Lost in the thoughts of gobbling them down, he enjoyed his hurried return journey. His mother would be home, and she would surely pack a haversack full of them.

And he was right. He did find mother home. But the scene was not what he had expected. He found mother Durga eating from a bowl of rice. The eating was not disturbing. What was more disturbing was the way she ate. She was gobbling down the rice as if she had never eaten before. Not with two hands but all ten hands. Ganesha was flabbergasted. He couldn't understand his mother's behaviour. Worried, he hastened towards her to find out the cause of her anxiety.

"Mother, why are you gulping down rice like this?" he asked trying to stop her from swallowing another mouthful.

Durga began to weep. She said, "Once you are married, your wife may not give me enough food to eat. So, I'm eating all I can now."

Ganesha broke into tears. Insecurities can create havoc in life. Just comforting her would not be enough. He had to come up with a long-term solution. As he pacified her, he kept thinking. Then he went out into the garden and searched for a banana tree. That would make the perfect daughter-in-law for his mother.

Carrying it inside with ease, he said, "Mother, this is your daughter-in-law. Now you need not worry at all." A dutiful and loving son Ganesha had eased his mother's trauma, assuring her that she would always be taken care of.

This is a legend popular in West Bengal. During Durga Puja, devotees dress a banana tree like a bride and call it *Kola Bou.* The trunk is draped in a white saree with red border, while the leaves sport vermilion. The tree is also smeared with sandal wood paste. The ritual is to place the tree on a pedestal and worship it with incense and by showering flowers. The tree is always placed on Ganesha's right, the rightful place of a wife. The puja celebrates Ganesha as a dutiful and loving son, always eager to care for his mother.

Source – Folk Tales

25.
THE SIGNIFICANCE OF DURVA GRASS

Ashraya, the wife of Sage Kaundinya, was on her way to heaven to meet Indra. It was not as if she wanted to go, but her husband had sent her. His instructions had made no sense to her. But he never did anything without a purpose. All she had done was ask him a question. And that had resulted in her taking this journey to the heavenly planets.

Sage Kaundinya was a highly learned scholar. His daily practice was the elaborate worship of Lord Ganesha. This involved the recitation of many chants and hymns glorifying the deity. Along with that, he offered Durva grass on Ganesha's head every day, without fail. Without the offering of Durva grass, his worship was never complete. It was an integral part of the ritual to the extent that he would not start the prayer until he had the Durva grass. Every morning, Ashraya, his wife, collected fresh grass from the field for his offering. Luckily, Durva was abundantly available, so it was never a difficult task to procure it.

One day, when the sage was in the middle of his midday meal, she asked him, "Why is it so important to offer Durva grass to Ganesha . . . how can an ordinary grass which is not mentioned in any scriptures be so important for Ganesha?"

And her query was quite valid. Durva was ordinary from any angle you saw. Yet, for Sage Kaundinya it was the most precious thing he could offer to Ganesha. Why?

It was not the first time she had expressed her curiosity about this. She had asked him many times before. And to his credit, he had answered her every time. He had told her how Ganesha had swallowed the fire demon Analasura and how the demon, once inside Ganesha's stomach, had continued to blow out fire to make him uncomfortable; how Ganesha found the heat unbearable and was desperate to cool himself. And when nothing worked, it was the Durva grass offered to him by sages that had finally eased his fiery distress.

Even after hearing this story repeatedly, Ashraya was still not convinced. If only she could get to the bottom of why Durva was so important . . .

"Please go to Indra with these twenty-one bunches of Durva grass and ask him to exchange it for gold."

Ashraya was surprised. She looked at him, trying to decipher what was going on in his mind. But his blank countenance gave her no clue. She knew it was connected to her badgering him for answers and he had found a way to make her see.

Almost reluctantly, she got up and collected the Durva bundles, and then left. It was a long journey and she finally arrived at the paradise court of King Indra.

"Sage Kaundinya has sent me to exchange these twenty-one bundles of Durva grass for gold, by weight," she requested Indra.

Indra did not think it was an unusual request. Nor did he think it was implausible. He simply asked her to contact Kubera, his treasurer, who would do the needful.

Ashraya sought Kubera and repeated what she had told Indra. Sage Kaundinya was well-known in all the planets, so no one questioned her. If the sage wanted something, it would be done, no questions asked. He took her to his inner chamber and placed all the Durva bundles on one side of the weighing scale. On the other side he put gold that he thought would be sufficient in weight. But the Durva side remained heavier. Some more gold was required. Kubera topped the pan with more gold, but the other side still did not move even a millimetre. He added even more gold, and then some more. He went on adding gold until there was a mountain of gold and yet the insignificant Durva remained heavier than all of it.

A flabbergasted Kubera stared at his weighing scale, scratching his head. He added more and more gold till his treasury was empty. His treasury was empty! The words kept echoing in his mind. His treasury was empty. Yet it was not equivalent to twenty-one bundles of Durva grass. He had to escalate the matter to Indra.

Taking Ashraya along, they went to see Indra. Kubera explained to him how he was unable to meet Sage Kaundinya's instruction. They simply did not have enough gold to equal the Durva grass. Supremely puzzled, Indra hurried to see the weighing scale. Indeed, the Durva-bearing pan was heavier than all the gold in his kingdom.

There was only one person who could solve this mystery. Sage Kaundinya. It was he who had sent his wife Ashraya with this impossible task of weighing the Durva grass. He alone could explain what was going on.

Ashraya took both Indra and Kubera back home to meet her husband. Feigning surprise, the sage welcomed them. He of course was expecting them to come, knowing very well that they would never be able to outweigh the value of Durva grass. The grass was, after all, invaluable. Beyond compare. So precious that Ganesha kept it on his head. And yet, his wife could not understand this simple fact. And that is why he had to plan this elaborate scheme so she could see it with her own eyes that nothing could match its weight, not even gold.

He patiently explained the glories of Durva to them and that it was so priceless that Ganesha was always pleased when it was offered. The fact that it was important to Ganesha, and that Ganesha loved it, gave Durva the topmost position that it enjoyed. Gold was too petty in front of love.

Source – Mudgala Purana

26.
THE STORY OF SANKASHTHI CHATURTHI

Lord Shiva would sometimes go into deep meditation for days together. When he was absorbed in it, neither the snow-clad mountains nor the freezing frosty winds could make any impact on him. Weeks and months passed but his meditation continued uninterrupted. The fire of his inner energy drenched him in sweat.

One day, a drop of his divine sweat fell off his body. The drop of sweat was as full of vitality and energy as Shiva himself. Something divine happened to the drop. From Mount Kailash, it tumbled towards the earth. As soon as it came in touch with

Mother Earth, a divine child was born. A child as fiery as Lord Shiva himself.

When Lord Shiva saw the birth of the child in Mother Earth's womb, he placed the child in her cradle, giving her the responsibility of looking after his upbringing. Mother Earth was only too happy to raise him as her own. She was, after all, a mother.

Like all mothers she nurtured the child dreaming of giving him the best education. And that meant learning from exalted sages. Amongst sages, one name flashed prominently in her mind, that of Sage Bhardwaj. He would be the ideal person to guide her precious son.

She quickly approached him and gave him her son's background. Sage Bhardwaj accepted her request to take the boy under his wing and give him a good education. He named him Bhauma, or son of Bhumi (earth). Sage Bhardwaj became known as the father of Bhauma.

Bhauma proved to be a diligent child. From a young age, he developed a deep fascination verging on obsession for Lord Ganesha. As he grew up to become learned, his devotion for Ganesha grew too, consistently. One day he went to his father and asked him for a mantra which could further his devotion to Lord Ganesha. He was desperate to please his charming lord. If only he could get his vision and blessings, his life would be worthwhile.

Sage Bhardwaj respected Bhauma's spiritual desires and gave him a mantra. He also instructed him to go to the banks of River Narmada, the perfect place to observe austerities and invoke his deity.

Bhauma listened to all the instructions attentively and followed them precisely. For many years, he remained absorbed in Lord Ganesha, chanting the mantra given by his guru and father. Years rolled by in intense austerities. Young Bhauma's determination and dedication were unflinching. Pleased by Bhauma's intensity of desire to see him, Lord Ganesha had no option but to appear in front of him.

It was the fourth day of the waxing moon of the lunar month of Magh, and a Tuesday, when Bhauma was blessed by Ganesha. Bhauma cried in ecstasy when he saw the majestic form of Ganesha. His long-cherished dream had come true. Ganesha blessed him and granted him a boon. But Bhauma wanted nothing more after receiving Ganesha's divine darshan.

"I'm happy to get your darshan, this is enough

for me," was his humble reply. "My birth and life have been purified."

But Ganesha could not return without bestowing a boon on his disciple.

"May you always be so blissful and devoted! But please ask for a boon. I cannot return without giving. Ask without hesitation," he encouraged Bhauma.

"I am a mere mortal, O' Ganesha. But I do wish that whenever you are remembered, I too be remembered with you."

Ganesha had no hesitation in accepting the request. He blessed Bhauma saying, "Because of your fiery red colour, I give you the name Angarak. You will be a learned sage and go by the name of Sage Angarak. From now on you are the presiding deity of planet Mars (mangal), which is worshipped every Tuesday.

"The Sankashthi Chaturthi, which is always on a Tuesday, will be henceforth known as Angarak Chaturthi. Fasting on Angarak Chaturthi will mean getting my blessings."

This is how both Mars and Sankashthi got associated with Sage Angarak. Devotees of Ganesha fast and pray for his blessings on that day.

Source - Ganesha Purana

27.
THE STORY OF THE GOKARNA SHIVA LINGA

Ravana, the king of Lanka, was lost in his own thoughts. Lately he had been thinking of how to make himself more powerful than ever. So powerful that he no longer feared anyone. This required him to perform austerities. Because he was looking for something extraordinary, his austerities too would have to be extraordinary.

There was something else troubling him. Every now and then, he had to go to Mount Kailash to seek boons from Shiva. Shiva's abode was in the far north and he was in the extreme south. It required a great deal of time and energy to reach there. He had already attempted once before to lift Mount Kailash and bring it back to Lanka. This had angered Shiva so much that he tapped the mountain with his foot and Ravana's fingers got trapped under the mountain. Apart from the immense pain, he had to perform penance for a thousand years and compose beautiful verses in glory of Lord Shiva to appease him. Only then he was able to return to Lanka.

Now he was a little hesitant to take that journey back to Kailash and face Shiva again. Moreover, his mother did not have a personal Shiva *lingam* to worship. Every day she would build one with sand and it would get washed away by the ocean. She had requested Ravana to ask Shiva for a lingam for her to worship. So, this made it necessary for him to go back. He had promised her that he would bring her the main *atmalingam* for her to worship. While he was there, he would again ask Shiva to protect his kingdom and himself from destruction. Having thus decided, he set off from Lanka. On the way, he constantly prayed to Lord Shiva for forgiveness, because he did not want anything to go wrong. Many a times Vishnu and Saraswati were known to play tricks and fool the demons into asking for the wrong things, things they had not even wanted.

To please Lord Shiva, Ravana began a series of austerities. Time passed. But Shiva did not make an appearance. Devastated by his failure, Ravana decided to cut off his heads one by one. He even made a *veena* (musical instrument) from them to sing hymns to please the lord. It was only when he had chopped nine of his heads did Shiva make an appearance. Ravana sighed in relief. Now that Shiva was pleased, he asked for the two things he had come for.

"O' kind Lord Shiva. Please make me and my kingdom indestructible so that whoever attacks me can never win. Also please give me your atmalingam so that my mother can worship you."

Lord Shiva had no hesitation in fulfilling both of Ravana's wishes. He gave him his powerful atmalingam and said, "Take this *Jyotirlinga.* It will serve both purposes. Its presence will make you invincible and it will satisfy your mother's desire as well. But remember, you must walk back to Lanka holding it very carefully and wherever you place it down, it will stay there. It cannot be moved once it's put down. So be very careful and very sure before putting it down."

Shiva's words were music to Ravana's ears. In great ecstasy, he accepted the lingam and started the arduous journey back home to his golden Lanka. He couldn't wait to get back and rule the whole universe without the fear of defeat or death.

The only impediment was that he had to walk. He walked as fast as he could, conscious of the fact that he was holding the venerable lingam in his hands. He did not have the luxury to stop anywhere or even take a bio break. How could he? So, he just did the best he could and stayed on his path.

When the demigods heard the news that Ravana had received the boon of being indestructible and invincible, they nearly fainted. He was dangerous now. What would he become once the lingam was installed in Lanka? They shuddered in fear at the very thought. They approached Ganesha and asked him if he could do something about it. Ganesha too was sceptical about Ravana being bestowed with the boon and assured the gods he would find a way out.

Meanwhile, the sun was setting and Ravana had covered half the distance. It was time for his evening ablutions which were mandatory for him. But how could he put the precious lingam down? It was meant to be placed in Lanka. He looked around him for help. He spotted a young cowherd who seemed lost in his own world. Could he trust him to hold his treasure and not run away with it? He seemed innocent enough. Moreover, what choice did he have? He called out to the boy and asked him to hold the lingam till he returned. The boy very innocently nodded his head and said, "I need to run home soon so if you get delayed, I will call out to you thrice and then put this lingam down."

Ravana quickly agreed without even fully registering what the boy said. He just wanted to finish his ablutions and be on his way. Little did he realise that the boy was none other than Ganesha himself. Ganesha had just been waiting for an opportunity to lay his hands on the lingam. After a few minutes, Ganesha called out thrice to Ravana. There was no reply. He quickly put the lingam down citing he was tired and he needed to go.

When Ravana returned, he got the shock of his life. The lingam he had sacrificed his heads for, the lingam that was to make him invincible, that lingam that was so close to his destination . . . he had lost it! Like a dead duck, he sank to the ground in total despair. Staring wildly at the boy, he tried to punch him on his head. But that didn't help one bit. He tried to uproot the lingam. He used all his might and he tried and he tried, but the lingam would just not budge. Eventually he gave up, accepting defeat in disgust. He turned around to see the cowherd boy also disappearing underground along with his cows. He somehow managed to catch the ears of the last cow. This place was thus called Gokarna or ears of cow. The lingam established in Gokarna was named Mahabaleshwar, meaning "all powerful". The deity of Ganapati in the temple has a dent on its head indicating the punch given by Ravana.

Irrespective of whether you are good or bad, if you are willing, divinity is always available to everyone. But whether you make it a curse or a boon for yourself is left to your inherent nature. What kind of attitude and mind you cultivate within yourself determines how you make use of your existence.

Source – Shiva Purana

28.
HOW THE PEACOCK BECAME GANESHA'S VEHICLE

Ganesha loved mangoes. As much as he did bananas. And grapes. Actually, he loved all sweet and juicy things. But when mangoes were in season, topmost on his mind were delicious mangoes. So much so that he and his friends played in a mango orchard all day.

One day his friends decided to eat the mangoes. Trees laden with golden mangoes was a sight they just could not resist. Ganesha consented and they all jumped on the tree. Plucking as many mangoes as they could, they stuffed their mouths with mango pulp. Mango juice flowed out from the corners of their mouth as they merrily sucked them. The collective slurping and sucking sounded like a gigantic demon at work.

Once the boys had feasted on the king of fruits to their hearts' content, they started throwing the mangoes at each other, getting wilder and wilder with every passing moment. To make matters worse, one mango accidentally went and hit a woman. This woman had been guarding some eggs. As soon as she got hit, she let out a loud painful moan scaring the boisterous boys. They had not even known she was there. She was Vinata, wife of Sage Kashyapa. The eggs were all her babies, and she was protecting them from getting hurt.

The boys, including Ganesha, hid themselves in fear when she enquired angrily who had hit her. Ganesha was closest to the egg that she was guarding and was most likely to get caught by her. Showing amazing agility, he jumped into a hole in the trunk of a tree. To his surprise, he collided with another egg kept safely in hiding.

Afraid that he may have damaged the egg, he touched it to make sure. No sooner had he touched it, the egg cracked open. Out came a huge bird that was even bigger than Ganesha, even at birth. It flapped its wings in panic and tried to get Ganesha out of the way thinking him to be an enemy. Ganesha was worried that the monstrous bird may actually damage Vinata's eggs, and he would be blamed for it. He caught the bird with both his hands and jumped out of the trunk. Keeping control over the bird, he mounted it.

Relieved that no damage was done, he looked towards Vinata, the sage's wife. Vinata walked towards him with folded hands and said earnestly, "This peacock is also the son of Sage Kashyapa. Please accept him as your vehicle. The sage had prophesised that whoever breaks the egg would be the peacock's master."

Ganesha was glad to accept a vehicle for himself. A grand peacock that could take him for many a joy ride. He thanked Vinata and joined his friends again to continue from where they had left off.

Source – Mudgala Purana

29.
ANOTHER LEGEND ABOUT HOW GANESHA GOT HIS ELEPHANT HEAD

Curiosity is an inherent aspect of all living entities. Narada muni, especially, was known for his never-ending curiosity. No wonder he is described as the first journalist in human history, who recognised the power of communication and news. His very name suggests the role he played; 'Naar' means wisdom and 'da' means giver. With his intelligent curiosity, he was a storehouse of wisdom.

He had just bumped into Ganesha while travelling in space. He loved Ganesha as he was so unlike other gods. Right from his physical appearance (he had the head of an elephant) to his intellectual prowess (that superseded many others). He simply stood out. Everyone loved him. After all, he was the one to turn to in times of trouble. His auspicious remembrance removed all obstacles.

But wait a minute. Amongst all these thoughts that were streaming, there was some discrepancy. He couldn't understand it—if Ganesha could remove all obstacles, why did he not save his head? His elephant head was testimony to the fact that he could not overcome the obstacles in his own life. How could he then help others?

Once this thought entered Narada muni's mind, he became restless. He had to get to the bottom of the mystery behind this. How he loved such mysteries! It gave him an opportunity to travel and meet Lord Narayana and find out more details about what happened, why it happened, etc. The more the information, the more useful it proved in dealing with people.

He quickly changed his course and headed to Vaikuntha. He would learn the truth from Lord Narayana.

Narayana was not at all surprised to see Narada entering his abode. It would be a surprise if he did not show up for a couple of days. He was conspicuous by his absence and then Narayana would wonder what was keeping him so busy that kept him from visiting him. Whenever He saw Narada heading towards him, He was assured that all was well with him and the world at large.

"O' Lord Narayana," exclaimed Narada, his eyes lighting up in sheer joy. His energy was infectious. The darshan of his Lord Narayana gave him such a thrill that it felt as though someone had plugged him into a high-powered socket. After the round of preliminary etiquette, he came to the point.

"Ganesha is Vignesha. Remover of all impediments. And yet, when it came to himself, he suffered tremendously to the extent of losing his head. How strange is that? The one who removes all impediments had to go through an impediment."

Narayana was impressed with Narada's logic. No one had ever thought of this till today. Unable to bear Lord Narayana's silence even for a moment, Narada urged Him to reveal the secret and end the suspense. Amused at Narada's impatience, the Lord decided to indulge him. After all, he was His beloved devotee who travelled non-stop to preach the glories of the Lord.

"My dear Narada, the story is very interesting. And it all dates back to before Ganesha was even born. So, it has nothing to do with him. He was simply a victim."

Now Narada was all ears. This was too interesting! He inched closer to Lord Narayana lest he missed out on a single word.

"Long ago there existed two demons called Mali and Sumali. As all demons are, they were also daredevils, experts in destruction and creating mayhem. Normally, gods in the heavenly world expect that from demons. But these two were a class apart. Their antics took many lives and disturbed many worlds. Why was it that no one could stop them?"

Narayana looked at Narada, waiting for an answer. Narada shrugged his shoulders. Usually, the heavenly residents found some way to stop the demons. But here they seemed powerless.

"It was because both were staunch devotees of Lord Shiva. If they had not been empowered by

Lord Shiva, something could be done. But in front of Lord Shiva's boons, the demigods didn't stand a chance."

Narada nodded enthusiastically. This was nothing new. These demons knew all the tricks of the trade to get boons that gave them what they asked for. If not immortality, then it was something close to it. As much as a mongoose loves snakes, demons love deathlessness.

"Tolerance has its limits. And one day Suryadeva reached his capacity of tolerance. Unmindful of the consequences, he attacked the devil duo Mali and Sumali. Shiva, being duty-bound, had to protect his devotees and he attacked Suryadeva with his trident. Naturally, Suryadeva could not survive the lethal attack. He fell unconscious, very close to death. His falling resulted in a natural disaster. The sun set all over the universe. Darkness spread its wings causing fear and lamentation. When Sage Kashyapa came to know that his precious son had been attacked with malicious intentions, he lost his cool.

"He immediately reached the scene of the crime and caught Lord Shiva. Seething with anger, he hurled a curse at him. 'How dare you attack Surya and throw the whole world into a web of darkness! Just as you pierced my son with your trident, I curse you that your son's head will also be severed with a sharp weapon. You will pay for your reckless and thoughtless ways!'

"His words hit Lord Shiva like a brick, and he realised the gravity of his mistake. He had caused more chaos by throwing the world into total darkness. Additionally, he had invited serious trouble for his own son. The least he could do was revive Suryadeva and end the darkness. Immediately, he got into action and soon, Suryadeva was up and upright again. The world heaved a sigh of relief. Their beloved sun was back. Kashyapa heaved a sigh of relief too. His son was back.

"Because Sage Kashyapa's curse would fructify sooner or later, Shiva expedited the curse by severing Ganesha's head and giving him an elephant head."

The secret was out and Narada broke into a broad smile. What a story! There was no way Ganesha could have stopped this from happening. In fact, because he was Vigneshwar, the curse had passed off without any catastrophe taking place.

No real damage was done, and his unusual head had turned into a unique feature that attracted both children and adults alike.

Narada thanked Lord Narayana as he continued his journey, lost in thoughts of the twists and turns of life where a curse had turned Ganesha and his persona into an all-time favourite god.

Source – Folk Tales

30.
THE STORY OF GANESHA'S MISSING TUSK

Narada had gone a considerable way when suddenly he had another doubt. Should he turn and go back and have it clarified, he wondered. It was a trifle embarrassing to go and ask. Just as he was about to talk himself out of it, he remembered some verses from the *Bhagavad Gita* where Krishna is addressed as Madhusudana, slayer of doubts. If doubts are not taken care of, they become as destructive as demons. His mind now made up, he headed back again towards Vaikuntha.

If Lord Narayana was surprised to see him back so soon, He did not show it. Would anything ever surprise Him, Narada wondered. He knows everything anyway.

"I thought of another question," Narada explained to Him, "and so I had to return."

The Lord simply smiled, encouraging him to ask.

"When the elephant's head was placed on Ganesha, it had two tusks. Now Ganesha has only one. What happened to the missing tusk?"

Although Narada did not say it explicitly, Lord Narayana understood the implication. His doubt had not been dispelled yet. What he really meant was how did Ganesha manage to lose his tooth? Why wasn't he able to protect himself?

"Narada muni, I will tell you what happened and how Ganesha fearlessly faced the mighty warrior Parshuram."

Narada settled down comfortably at the feet of Lord Narayana to soak in the bliss.

"Parshuram's anger was at its peak when his father, the great Sage Jamadagni, was killed by the Kshatriya King Kartaviryarjuna. Parshuram took the vow of terminating the entire Kshatriya clan to avenge his death. He travelled the world a number of times and ruthlessly killed many of them. Imagine his strength and valour. Single-handedly eliminating Kshatriyas who themselves were known for their aggression. However, Parshuram was aggressive way beyond them. And after his thirst for revenge had been quenched, he decided to visit his guru Lord Shiva for his blessings and wishes.

"But imagine his surprise when he reached Mount Kailash and was not allowed to enter. The gate that always welcomed him in the past was being guarded by a puny half-human half-elephant. He had dared to stop the mighty Parshuram. His body trembled in anger at this high level of insult. Brave kings shuddered when he appeared whereas this little boy was trying to stop him from entering without any inkling of the consequences.

"Not that little Ganesha was being disrespectful to Parshuram. He was so polite and well-mannered that he would never disrespect even an ant. All he had requested Parshuram was to not disturb his parents who were resting at that time. It wasn't even an unusual request. Only an insensitive person would want to wake up someone who was sleeping. And that too disturbing your guru?

"Parshuram, because he was so incensed at being stopped, could not think straight to comprehend that Ganesha was not really stopping him but only asking him not to disturb his parents."

Narada agreed. Anger took away all capacity to think rationally and caused you to do stupid things. He was eager to know what Parshuram did next.

"Parshuram refused to hear anything that Ganesha said. Instead, he thundered in a voice loud enough to kill the weak hearted instantly. 'Don't you know who I am? I am the one who has killed all the evil Kshatriyas on earth. You think you have the power to stop me?' He smirked and pushed Ganesha aside to forcefully enter the holy mountain. Ganesha resisted and what followed was a scuffle between them. Neither allowing the other to move. Parshuram tried to raise his axe, the weapon that he always carried with him. The same axe that he had literally slaughtered the Kshatriyas with.

"But before he could even move a muscle, with lightning speed Ganesha wrapped his trunk around him and flung him far, far away. He ended up falling inside the sea as if dropped like a ball. Before he could emerge out of there, Ganesha picked him up once again and flung him on the ground elsewhere. He played with Parshuram for a while like a cat plays with a mouse.

"In between, Parshuram managed to hurl his axe at Ganesha. Caught off guard, Ganesha's response came a little too late. The axe had done the damage. It had broken his left tusk. This was not an ordinary tusk. When it hit the ground, it made a huge impact. The sound echoed across the universe, startling Shiva and Parvati. They woke up with a jerk, trying to figure out the source of sound.

"Parvati first thought of Ganesha. Was he safe? She rushed out to see a sight that sank her heart; her child was bleeding with a broken tusk. Then she saw Parshuram. No words were needed for her to understand what had transpired. She instinctively hugged her hurt child as she glanced with contempt at Parshuram.

"After ensuring that Ganesha was not in any danger, she spoke to Parshuram. 'My son Ganesha is capable of defeating the most powerful of living beings. It is his sensitivity that he has not harmed you or shown you his strength in a damaging way. He has never even hurt a fly in his life. Yet, you attacked him and hurt him.'

"Parshuram was now turning red with embarrassment. His anger had carried him away again. He asked for forgiveness. But Ganesha's tusk had been broken, giving him the title of Ekadanta or single-tusked."

Lord Narayana ended the story, quelling all the doubts of Narada muni, with this statement, "Ganesha's power to handle impediments comes from his own mental strength."

Source – Brahma Vaivarta Purana

31.
THE EIGHT INCARNATIONS OF GANESHA

Lord Ganesha is unique. Consider his looks—he sports an elephant's head and a potbelly. His vehicle? He mounts a mouse in most of his incarnations! A very unlikely vehicle! It's difficult to be inspired by someone who appears on a mouse, isn't it? It's like a superhero on a mission to save the world riding a broken-down two-wheeler. But save the world he does, in style, that too. Eight of his incarnations are most popular, appearing in different cosmic yugas. Each incarnation is on a mission to annihilate one of the eight weaknesses humans possess.

As Vakratunda, he battles jealousy. As Ekadanta, he hits against arrogance. As Mahodara, it is delusion. Gajavaktra (Gajanana) defeats the demon of greed. Lambodara attacks anger while Vikata, Vighnaraja, and Dhoomravarna stamp out lust, intoxication, and ego. All in all, this amazing son of Shiva is loved by all because remembering him ensures success and prosperity.

Vakratunda

Ganesha with a twisted trunk or Vakratunda is the first incarnation. Matsarasura was a jealous demon who acquired huge powers thanks to the blessings of Lord Shiva. On a winning spree, he conquered the three worlds and the demon guru Shukracharya proclaimed him as the king of asuras. When the devatas asked Lord Shiva for protection, Matsarasura went and defeated Lord Shiva also.

Finally, Ganesha came to the rescue in Vakratunda avatara and assured the devatas of protection. Matsarasura turned turtle as soon as he saw Vakratunda. He surrendered at his feet without a fight. Vakratunda forgave him and returned the glory of the heavenly planets to the devatas.

Ekdanta

Ekdanta is Ganesha's incarnation with a single tusk and four hands. He fought against the demon Madasura, the embodiment of arrogance. Madasura was the son of Sage Chyavan and the pupil of Shukracharya. By performing penance for thousands of years, Madasura received a sublime boon from Shakti that all his desires would be fulfilled. Thereafter, he was crowned as king of Triloka, and gained victory over kings and gods. He was nothing short of a terrorist.

Under his rule, all virtuous qualities disappeared from the universe. Only when the gods invoked Ekadanta on Sanat Kumar's advice, Madasura was cut to size by Ekdanta's axe. He became unconscious and when he came back to his senses, he knew he was no match for the mighty incarnation of Lord Ganesha. Ekadanta instructed him that he should never be seen in the vicinity of his devotees. Thus, Ekadanta worship brings auspiciousness and removal of all obstacles.

Mahodara

Mohasura was a demon seeped in delusion and confusion. His guru Shukracharya gave him a mantra to please the Sun god. Once he pleased the Sun god, he bullied all the devatas. The terrified devatas prayed to Lord Ganesha who decided to help them and appeared as Mahodara. The sight of Mahodara inspired Shukracharya to direct his pupil to surrender to Mahodara and not incur his wrath. Lord Shiva sang glories of Mahodara to convince the demon of Mahodara's power. Mohasura accepted defeat and retreated to Pataal loka.

Gajanana

Lobhasura, the demon of greed, was defeated by Gajanana. Lobhasura was born from Kubera, the treasurer of gods. Once when Kubera was visiting Mount Kailash, he felt lusty desire for the beautiful Parvati. When Parvati was enraged, Kubera shivered in fear and from that fear came Lobhasura. Lobhasura went on to become king of the demons with the blessings of Shukracharya. Lord Shiva too blessed him with fearlessness.

Armed with the boon, Lobhasura unleashed great cruelty and torture on all living beings, including sages and devatas. Not even afraid of Lord Shiva, he turned his attention to Mount Kailash and displaced Lord Shiva. Shiva gave up his abode under the demonic threat. The devatas approached Raibhya muni who advised them to call upon Lord Ganesha. He arrived as Gajanana and sent a message via Lord Shiva to Lobhasura demanding his surrender. Shiva advised Lobhasura to be wise and surrender to Gajanana rather than face certain defeat. Gauging Gajanana's strength, Lobhasura thought it was wiser to surrender to a power superior to him. He begged for forgiveness and returned to Pataal loka.

Lambodara

The much-loved Lambodara has a huge potbelly because within it reside the multiple universes inhabited by infinite living creatures. His belly is large enough to carry the entire world within. He incarnated to annihilate the demon of anger, Krodhasura. Once Lord Vishnu took the form of Mohini, a beautiful girl. Unfortunately, Lord Shiva was angry about not being present there to see the unusual divine beauty of Lord Vishnu. From his frustration was born Krodhasura.

Krodhasura lived a demonic life having been blessed by the Sun god. Finally, his rule came to an end with the advent of Lambodara Ganesha. Krodhasura realised that his stature was too low to fight against Lambodara and gave up his ambition of ruling the heavens.

Vikata

Vikata came riding on a peacock to subdue the demon of lust, Kamasura. Blessed by Shiva and under the tutelage of Shukracharya, Kamasura conquered the three worlds. He married Trishna, daughter of Mahishasura, and had two sons, Soshana and Dushpoora. Ravana was the chief commander of his army. The devatas, freaked out by the demon's atrocities, approached Maharishi Mudgal who could only advise them to beseech Lord Ganesha. Ganesha incarnated as Vikata on a peacock. A fierce battle ensued between the demon and Vikata Ganesha. Kamasura dropped unconscious unable to bear Vikata's attack. When he became conscious, he also came to his senses and asked for forgiveness. The rescued gods rejoiced and danced and named their saviour Mayureshwar.

Vighnaraja

This is the most popular form of Ganesha as the remover of all obstacles. Equally surprising is his vehicle, a serpent. Parvati was once in a jovial mood, laughing with her friends in the celestial garden. From her laughter was born a handsome male form. He prostrated in front of her as she was his mother. When he asked her what she wanted him to do, Parvati replied that he should stay in a jungle and meditate on Lord Ganesha. She also gave him a name—Mama. Mama left obediently to do as instructed. On the way he was accosted by a demon Sambara, who lured him into joining the demonic cult. Mama was influenced and he became part of the demonic tribe, following their ways. In course of time, the angelic Mama became the king of demons Mamasura. When his atrocities grew out of proportion, Ganesha appeared on the serpent and Vighnaharta Ganesha subdued Mamasura establishing peace and harmony once again.

Dhumravarna

Aham means ego, a demonic force that grips the mind and never lets go. Aham is so deeply embedded in the human psyche that it takes a demonic form and is known as Ahamkasura. He was born from the sneeze of the Sun god when the Sun god was seized with the thought that he was the governor of all worlds. As soon as he sneezed, Ahamkasura came out. He travelled to the world of demons, wedded Mamta, and had two sons Garva and Shreshta. Finally, his tyranny was put to an end by Dhumravarna Ganesha.

Source – Mudgala Purana

32.
THE MEANING AND SIGNIFICANCE OF GANESHA'S DIVINE FORM

Ganesha, Ganapati, Vinayaka, Vighnaharta, Pillaiyar, or Ekadanta, is one of the most popular and loved gods in Hindu culture. While Ganesha is popular in North India, Ganapati is preferred in South India, as head of the ganas. Names like Ekdanta and Pillaiyar are derived from his appearance (*danta* means tooth and *pella* means tusk). Vighnaharta refers to his title as the Lord of Obstacles. He is also the god of intelligence and wisdom. Destroyer of selfishness and pride. The Lord of new beginnings, who blesses and provides a path of ease.

Maharashtra is the most popular state of worship for Ganesha. Here, the most important places of Ganesha worship are the eight religious sites around Pune called the Ashtavinayaks (eight Vinayaks). The eight temples are called Moreshwar Temple, Siddhivinayak Temple, Ballaleshwar Temple, Varadavinayak Temple, Chintamani Temple, Girijatmaj Temple, Vighnahar Temple, and Mahaganapati Temple. In all these temples, the deities of Ganesha are made out of a single piece of rock and are hence said to be self-manifested.

He is depicted as four armed, holding his broken tusk in his lower right arm, a noose in the upper left hand, a bowl of modaks in his lower left hand, and an axe or goad in the upper right hand. Sometimes, the lower right hand doesn't hold the tusk, but is in *abhaya* mudra, providing protection to the devotee. His broken tusk, the result of fighting a demon or for writing the *Mahabharata*, is testimonial to his sacrifice and commitment to mankind.

The noose indicates that worldly desires and attachments are a noose, and he comes to liberate those in bondage of passion. The *ankush* or goad is to prod his followers along the path of righteousness and truthfulness.

Depending on the role he's playing, he may hold several other weapons as well. For destroying demons, common weapons are trident, spear, knife, bow, arrow, discus, sword, shield, mace, snake, hammer, large axe, pickaxe, battle axe, baton, conch, dagger, etc. In peaceful roles, he holds a pot of nectar, a pot of gems, prayer beads, a flower garland, a veena, fruits, grain, flowers, a lotus, a book, etc.

Ganesha stands apart because of his huge body that represents the cosmos. The large-sized body contains the whole universe and all living beings. Even more striking is his elephant head, symbolic of auspiciousness, strength, and intellectual prowess. Like the elephant, he is strong yet gentle. And is easily won over with love and kindness. He forgives just as easily too, moved by the affection of his devotees. Just like a single elephant is equivalent to a large army, Ganesha alone is enough to annihilate all demons.

The modaks and laddus are reminders of the sweetness he spreads amongst his devotees in terms of prosperity and wealth. His trunk mostly points to the left towards the sweets, showing his love for them.

His large ears represent listening to Vedic knowledge from the guru. The size of the ears is a subtle reminder to listen more and speak less. The ears also teach us to sift the bad from the good. After hearing, one needs to ponder for which a large head is needed. The eyes urge us to look into minute details. His trunk is symbolic of *viveka* or discrimination, the most important quality for progressing on the spiritual path.

The belly's advice is simple. Digest everything that comes, both good and bad things in life. The potbelly is sized that way because he devours all sorrows of his devotees. His voracious appetite comes from the fact that he can never be pleased by wealth. It is only love that quells his craving to eat.

Ganesha sometimes sports three eyes. The two eyes symbolise the power of Surya (the sun) and Chandra (the moon). The third eye at the centre of the forehead represents Agni, the god of fire. The forehead is the seat of wisdom.

Often Ganesha is seen decorated with the third day crescent moon on his head. Symbolically, this crescent leads to attaining pure knowledge and spiritual enlightenment.

He rides a mouse for two reasons. The nibbling mouse represents petty desires that nibble away into our spiritual core. The mouse is also an enemy of farmers, destroying crops. Ganesha heralds auspiciousness for farmers by keeping the mouse in check.

Every aspect of Ganesha has meaning and significance conveying his wisdom in the easiest possible ways.

Source – Ganesha Purana and Mudgala Purana

[illegible]

[illegible] knowledge [illegible]
[illegible] commitment.

[illegible]

[illegible]

[illegible]

SECTION 2:

Stories of Ganesha Temples

33.
VARAD VINAYAK TEMPLE

"I curse you to become a thorny *bhora* plant!"

Gritasamad cursed his own mother Mukunda and ran out of their hut with no idea of what he wanted to do next. The sun set simultaneously as if supporting the ominous curse. The surrounding darkness was simply an extension of the darkness in Gritasamad's heart. What else could there be? He had learnt a dark secret about himself. That he was not his father's son. He felt himself exploding into millions of tiny shrapnel and each shrapnel pierced him mentally, causing unbearable pain.

Mukunda had no option but to tell her son Gritasamad the truth. Sooner better than later. But now she wondered if she had done the right thing. She had lived with the burden of her past for far too long. Maybe the curse would give her the much-needed relief. Years ago, a young and handsome prince had walked into her husband's hut and walked out with her heart. It was Prince Rukmaganda, heir of Koudinyapur.

Born to King Bhima, legend was that his divine appearance and unwavering intelligence was a gift from the gods. No human could ever match his extraordinary persona. King Bhima had been childless, and he was just about to lose hope when Sage Vishwamitra advised him to meditate on a mantra. Prince Rukmaganda was a result of that penance. The prince visited this forest often and that's how he spotted Rishi Vachaknavi's hut and went in, hoping to get blessings from the sage.

As destiny would have it, the sage was out in the forest, immersed in meditation. His wife, Mukunda, welcomed the prince. It was love at first fight for the young Mukunda. She had fallen hard for him. So much so that she could not bear to see him go as he prepared to leave, when he learnt that the sage was not at home. In trying to prevent him from leaving, words gushed out of her mouth. Embarrassed yet helpless, she spoke her mind. "Young prince, your charm has enamoured my heart completely. Will you not fulfil my desires?"

A shocked Rukmaganda stopped dead in his tracks. Had he heard right or were his ears playing games? He turned back. The lusty look on the rishi's wife's face said it all. Rukmaganda was definitely aghast at the proposal, but he had to handle the situation delicately.

"It is not ethical for us to do that," he simply replied in a soft yet firm voice and walked back into the forest as quickly as his feet could carry him. Mukunda watched the well-toned youthful body as he disappeared from her view, silently willing him to turn back and return to her arms. But he didn't. Shattering all her hopes. Her heart was on fire and if the prince did not return to reciprocate her love, she wanted to burn in that fire itself. She waited with hope that he would realise his mistake and accept her. Minutes turned into hours. There was no sign of him. She paced restlessly, oscillating between thoughts of being in her lover's arms and burning herself in frustration.

Far above in the heavenly planets, Indra learnt of Mukunda's distress. Mukunda was beautiful. Perhaps he could satisfy her desires. Disguised as Rukmaganda, he came down to meet Mukunda. When Mukunda saw that Rukmaganda had returned, she went wild with joy and threw herself into his arms. Indra as Rukmaganda swooped her up in his arms and carried her inside. He fulfilled all her desires to her heart's content and then returned to heaven. A happy Mukunda had no inkling of the real identity of her lover. Even after he left, she had a smile on her face for days. Soon she gave birth to her son Gritasamad. Gritasamad was not her legitimate son, and this remained a well-kept secret. Until now.

On hearing the truth (which was not the whole truth), Gritasamad threw a curse at his mother. Shocked at the sudden turn of events, Mukunda hurled a counter curse.

"May you have a demon as a son!"

Immediately, there was a loud rumbling in the sky indicating there was more turbulence to come. This was followed by an aerial announcement. The alarmed mother-son duo looked up in wonder, astonished at hearing their names being called out from above. This was eerie as well as magical. What they heard was, "Mukunda, Gritasamad is the son of Indra!"

Now it was Mukunda's turn to be horrified. Since both had already cursed each other, there was nothing more to say. The next moment, Mukunda turned into a thorny bhora plant while Gritasamad sadly walked away into the forest. With a repentant heart, he sat under a tree to meditate on Ganesha to reverse his curse. There was nothing else he could think of under the circumstances.

Pleased with Gritasamad's devotion and sincerity, Ganesha appeared and blessed him. Aware that Gritasamad was troubled by his mother's curse, he gave him the boon that his son would never be defeated by anybody other than Lord Shiva.

On seeing Ganesha's divine form in front of him, Gritasamad experienced ecstasy. His world was a bubble holding only the two of them. He immediately thought how fortunate he was to see Ganesha first-hand. Eager to share his good fortune with others, he begged Ganesha to stay in the forest permanently. Ganesha's presence would mean that not only he but others too could always see him whenever they wanted to.

Happy to please his devotee, Ganesha obliged and accepted the offer to stay. Gritasamad busied himself in building a temple right there so that anyone who went through the forest could pray to Ganesha and get their wishes fulfilled.

The *swayambhu* deity came to be known as Varad Vinayak. It is said that there is a lamp in the temple that is burning continuously since 1892. Another belief is that by consuming the coconut *prasad* from the temple on Maghi Chaturdasi, one is sure to be blessed with a son. Thus, the temple sees many visitors in that month.

Source – Sthala Purana, Mudgala Purana

34.
THE STORY OF CHINTAMANI GANESHA

Before Gana began meditation and austerities to please Lord Shiva, he was a different boy. After he emerged from there, his personality was transformed. Born to Queen Gunavati and King Abhijit, he possessed all the royal qualities and more. Smart and strong, he was good material as heir to the throne. What transformed him were the boons he received from Lord Shiva.

As he sat in a meditative trance for days at a stretch, he suddenly snapped out of it when Lord Shiva appeared in front of him. Startled and at a loss for words, he was amazed to see the object of his meditation right in front of him and smiling. Prodded by Shiva, Gana asked for many boons that would make his life more opulent, royal, and fearless. Shiva granted him all that he asked and Gana returned to his kingdom, a happy man.

Everything changed for Gana after that. Gone was the gentle and good-hearted young man to be replaced by one who flaunted his wealth and power to anyone who dared to differ with him. He wanted absolute and total obedience. Shiva's boons had made him fearless to the extent of point-blank aggression and intolerance. Now that he knew he was undefeatable and powerful, his base nature took over. His ego blew up to gigantic proportions. He became insensitive and uncaring. This attracted bad company and soon Gana became known as a tyrannical spoilt brat.

One day, he and his army of goons headed towards Sage Kapila's ashram. They had heard that he possessed a *chintamani* gem and Gana wanted to verify the facts for himself. Now etiquette demanded that the sage welcome his guests and offer them food. Gana was not an ordinary guest but royalty.

He had to be served befitting a king. No ordinary person could possibly offer a royal feast to Gana and his army. But Sage Kapila was no ordinary sage. He was a maharishi. In the blink of the eye, he arranged for a lavish spread that would put even the royal kitchen to shame.

While the army chomped voraciously on the delicacies, Gana pondered. *How could a poor sage offer them something as magnificent as this?* Without showing any humility or respect for the sage, he demanded to know his secret. The sage had expected this because it was human nature. He also knew that once he gave out his secret, it would forcibly be taken away from him. But he decided to cross the bridge when he came to it. He could not possibly refuse to answer him now.

The sage said, "I have a gem, the chintamani, which fulfils everything I ask for. It's a desire-fulfilling gem given to me by the king of heavens, Lord Indra. When I asked for a lavish feast for the army, the gem created all of it."

Then he closed his eyes and sighed. Now the worst part would come. As expected, Gana demanded to see it. All humans were the same, thought the sage —greedy and selfish, wanting to snatch from others. Once he showed him the gem, he would forcibly take it away. And then he would use it, not for the welfare of mankind but for his own selfish grandeur.

Nonetheless, he still showed Gana the precious gem. Gana's eyeballs popped out and his mouth drooled as he eyed the unique stone. The sage quickly covered his jewel and took it back inside. Gana followed him inside and instructed the sage to hand it over to him. Kapila resisted but the strong lad pushed him aside and captured the jewel. Before the sage could react, he was gone, leaving a trail of destruction behind, ransacking the hut and all the plants in the vicinity.

Kapila muni calmly got up and cleared the mess. He had decided on his course of action. Meditation. One could move mountains with meditation. He meditated on Lord Ganesha asking for his help. Ganesha never missed an opportunity to help saintly people. He did not need to be told in words what the problem was and why the maharishi was seeking his help. He automatically knew.

For good people, Ganesha sometimes used soft techniques. Gana was not a bad person to begin with. He had pleased Shiva with his austerities, after all. Giving him the benefit of the doubt, Ganesha appeared to him in his dream. Gana dreamt that a fiercely angry Ganesha was beheading him. Instead of instilling fear, the dream had the opposite effect. How dare Sage Kaplia call Ganesha for help! Did he think he would get frightened by a dream?

Burning with rage, he immediately went to the muni's ashram to teach him a lesson. No one messed around with Gana. He was the fearless Gana who could defeat innumerable Ganeshas. Or so he thought. King Abhijit realised the dream indicated that Gana had gone too far this time. He even begged Gana to return the magical gem and not interfere with divine beings. But Gana had revenge on his mind. Taking his army with him, he stormed into the ashram, determined to end the story once and for all. To destroy one man against him and his army was a joking matter.

It is said that when the end is near, intelligence leaves your side. Gana too had overestimated himself and underestimated the sage's power who had the support of Ganesha's power. Ganesha and Siddhi Devi came to the ashram to protect the sanctity of the place and its people. Next, they created a thousand-armed warrior to fight on their behalf. Laksha, the warrior, had the strength and sense of both Ganesha and Siddhi. His thousand arms worked at a speed that was no match for Gana's soldiers. Before they could even open the attack, they were annihilated. Gana met the same fate. Who has ever tasted victory pitched against Ganesha?

Sage Kapila no longer desired to keep the chintamani in his possession. He offered it to Ganesha who readily accepted the gift. On Kapila's insistence, he stayed there under the Kadamba tree in the form of Chintamani Gaṇesha. It was under the Kadamba tree that Gana had been slayed.

Chintamani temple in Theur, Maharashtra is one of the Ashtavinayak temples.

Source – Mudgala Purana

35.
WHY LORD JAGANNATH DRESSES IN GANAPATI VESHA ON SNANA PURNIMA

Hot tears rolled down the cheeks of the pilgrim Ganapati Bhattar as he sat on the pavement facing the road leading to the Jagannath temple. Not just his eyes, but his heart was crying too. The pain of being backstabbed by those he trusted most was too much for him to bear. It wasn't really a person who had let him down but the revered *Puranas* that he had been reading all his life. He had always believed firmly that Lord Jagannath was the controller of the world and with his mercy anyone could be delivered. *Once I see Parambrahma Lord Jagannath with my eyes, my life will become successful.*

One day he read that Lord Jagannath had manifested in Nilgiri in His transcendental form as Daru Brahman. Immediately he was struck by an intense desire to see the Supreme Lord and fulfil his cherished dream of liberation. With no attachment to his material life, he was eager to see the transcendental Lord and attain moksha, never to return home to his village again. As his desire started building up, he could no longer stay at home. He was flooded with thoughts of renunciation and liberation. *My family is only a temporary relationship. They will abandon me once I become old and useless. Only brahman is a true friend.*

Inspired by such thoughts, he decided to leave home and visit Lord Jagannath, in the hope that His darshan would relieve him from the material world. He set off carrying nothing with him. It would be his last pilgrimage because the Lord's darshan would culminate in him getting moksha.

On the way, he ignored all hunger pangs, surviving on leaves and water. He ignored the blisters on his feet and felt no physical exhaustion; so consumed was he to get the Lord's darshan which would ultimately liberate him from the miseries of the material world. In this way, Ganapati Bhattar reached Atharnala bridge that connected the world to Puri and Jagannath temple. Whoever crossed this bridge would become free from facing Yamaraj at death.

Eager to purify himself before presenting himself to the Lord, he sat down to meditate on the Supreme Lord. When he came out of his reverie, it was evening, and many pilgrims were returning from the temple after darshan. Ganapati saw them holding pots of Jagannath prasad in their hands. Their walk and animated conversations interspersed by squeals of laughter suggested to him that they were very happy. *What could be making them so joyous?* he thought to himself.

Unable to control his curiosity, he stopped a traveller and asked him, "Please tell me, where are you coming from and what makes you so happy?"

The traveller replied, "What makes us so happy is the darshan of Jagannath. We spent two days in Puri and with great joy and contentment we are going back home."

Ganapati Bhattar was rather perplexed at the reply. He wanted to confirm and asked, "Have you really seen Param brahman?"

"Yes, we have seen Him," came the answer. Once the traveller had left his company, Ganapati sat down to absorb what he had just learnt. His confusion was that if they had seen brahman, they should have been liberated. That's what the *Puranas* said—that one achieves moksha after seeing the brahman, that is Lord Jagannath. Then how was it possible that the travellers were still on earth? Did that mean the *Puranas* were not stating the truth? Or was it that the travellers had seen some other deity and not the original brahman? His mind was reeling, unable to come to any conclusion. He doubted if he should visit Lord Jagannath at all if it was not going to help him achieve liberation.

He decided to ask a few more people to confirm. And sure enough, each one of them was returning after the darshan of brahman. Yet no one had been liberated. With this realisation, his shoulders drooped and tears rolled down his eyes.

With a heavy heart, he decided that there was no point in visiting the Lord because the *Puranas* had, after all, misled him into believing something else. If there was no liberation after getting darshan, then why go on living at all? All he wanted now was to leave his body then and there. He knew suicide was condoned in the scriptures, but his disappointment was so deep that he could not find any other way to deal with it.

As he sat there contemplating suicide, Lord Jagannath was feeling anxious. His devotee wanting to commit suicide and not wanting to meet Him was unthinkable. He desperately wanted Ganapati Bhattar to come and visit Him. Drastic situations call for drastic measures. So Jagannath disguised Himself as an old brahman and went to visit him.

"Why are you sitting here, looking so dejected with life? Tell me what is troubling you," the old brahman asked Ganapati Bhattar.

Ganapati Bhattar felt a surge of hope shoot through him, anticipating that help had come in the form of a learned brahman who would resolve his confusion and dilemma. He laid bare all his doubts in front of him.

"I read in the *Puranas* that one gets moksha after seeing Brahman, the Supreme Lord. However, after coming here, I realise that it's not true. This makes me very sad."

"Who said it's not true?" asked the brahman.

"I saw with my own eyes, travellers who had the darshan of Lord Jagannath going back home because they did not attain moksha. This proves Jagannath is not Brahman. Had Jagannath been the Param brahman, they would not be going back home," Ganapati explained his logic.

The wise old brahman said, "The Supreme Brahman is a desire-fulfilling tree, Kalpataru. He fulfils all desires. Is it not possible that those people who you met had no desire for moksha? They desired to go back home after darshan. So Jagannath had no option but to fulfil that desire and send them back home. If you go with any other desire, that desire will be fulfilled too."

Convinced with the brahman's argument, Ganapati Bhattar dropped the idea of suicide and entered Puri for the Lord's darshan. It was Snana Purnima, the day when Jagannath had to bathe before starting His ratha yatra. Lord Baldeva and Subhadra were accompanying Him, and the pujaris were pouring water over the three deities lovingly. The entire atmosphere was charged with cries of *Jai Jagannath!* Devotees stood there mesmerised in the presence of the Supreme Brahman. Even the demigods had descended, disguised as humans to see the divine scene.

But when Ganapati entered the Snana mandap and saw the Lord, his face fell. Again he had doubts. How could this be him? He had imagined the brahman to be his deity Ganesha. He had always worshipped Ganesha. Yet, it was not Ganesha who stood there but someone else. Where was his elephant-faced God?

Feeling let down yet again, he ran out of the temple, tears clouding his eyes. He had wanted to see Ganesha and only Ganesha and no one else. No one else could be God, he wailed silently.

As soon as Ganapati turned his back, Jagannath went into overdrive once again. How could He allow His devotee to leave without His darshan? This time Jagannath paid a visit to the king of Puri in his dream. He instructed the king to find the brahman called Ganapati Bhattar and bring him back to the temple. It was the king's responsibility to convince the brahman that he would indeed see the elephant-headed god he so loved.

King Mudiratha immediately ran to find Ganapati Bhattar. When he was found, he chastised him, "Why are you so foolish? How can you go back without taking darshan of the Supreme Lord, the Brahman? Please come with me and all your desires will be fulfilled. You can see Him as your elephant-headed god too."

Ganapati's body trembled and his lips quivered hearing what the king said. Everyone was forcing him to visit against his wishes. He shouted at the king, "He is not the Supreme God. Where is the elephant face? Stop cheating me. Why are you forcing me to go back?"

"Come with me and you will surely see the elephant face of Brahman," King Mudiratha said, pacifying the restless Ganapati.

Ganapati Bhattar could not refuse the offer, so he silently walked back to the temple. And there in front of him stood the lord, exactly how he had imagined him to be. With a trunk and a tusk. The beautiful elephant face he loved so much.

He quickly fell on the ground to offer his obeisance. Glorifying the lord, he said, "O' Gajanana, O' lord of the universe, now I can be content seeing your form. I have but one request. Whenever you come for a bath to Snana mandap, please display this form for darshan."

To fulfil his devotee's desire, Lord Jagannath acceded to his request and every year, he dresses in *hathi vesha* or Gajanana vesha or Ganapati vesha after the bath on Snana Purnima.

Source – Puranic Legends

36.
THE STORY OF THE MIRACULOUS KANIPAKAM VINAYAKA IN ANDHRA PRADESH

A thousand years ago there were three brothers. They were farmers. Life was tough, given that they were all handicapped. One was blind. Another was hearing impaired, and the third was speech impaired. Somehow, they worked together and managed to make a living on their farm. That year, their troubles compounded as they faced drought. There was no sign of water in their well. The once overflowing well was now showing its rock bottom. The villagers suggested they dig the well further and maybe they would reach a deeper water level.

Following the advice, one of the brothers entered into the well. He hit his iron axe intensely into it, but to his dismay, no amount of digging helped find water. He was about to give up when he heard a CLANK! His axe had hit not earth but something like metal. Why else would he hear the clanking sound? Intrigued, he peered closer. His brothers were standing outside the well, anticipating to hear or see the sound of gushing water.

But what he saw curdled his blood. A spout of fresh red blood sprang out from that location. The well was now filling with red blood instead of water. What followed next was a complete miracle. Or you could call it divine grace. He had been speech challenged since childhood but all of a sudden, he heard his own voice.

"Brothers, brothers, see what is happening."

He was frightened hearing the sound of his own voice. Was he hallucinating? Was he possessed? Who was speaking from inside him? Why so much blood? He couldn't make any sense of it. Afraid to see a well swelling with blood, he quickly clambered out of it. His brothers were there, waiting. They too seemed to be in a state of shock. And why not? They were all experiencing divine miracles they could never even dream of.

The blind brother could see, and the deaf brother could hear. One had gained instant vision, the other instant hearing. He had heard his brother screaming from the well and nearly fainted from the experience. The blind brother could clearly see the red well. All three of them held hands and started dancing in excitement. How it happened, they had no clue. For now, it did not matter. They could only revel in their good fortune.

Soon word spread about the miraculous happenings with the farmers and the well. Villagers thronged the well to witness the event with their own eyes. What a sight it was to see the jubilant brothers rejoicing and dancing around the well. And when they peeped inside, they were even more astonished. From the well emerged a self-manifesting *swayambhuva* idol of Lord Vinayaka. They offered coconuts and welcomed the deity. The deity remained inside the well. Blood gave way to crystal clear water, and everyone took the water as *tirtham*.

In the eleventh century, King Chola Kulothunga Chola-I had built a temple there which had been expanded in the fourteenth century by kings of the Vijayanagar dynasty. Known as the temple of Kanipakam Vinayaka (Andhra Pradesh), it is famous for many more miracles.

Swayambhuva Lord Vinayaka did not stop at just one miracle. He continues to show a miraculous phenomenon till today. Believe it or not, he continually grows in size. The deity expands in size practically on a daily basis, especially his knees and stomach. A silver *kavacham* or shield that was offered fifty years ago is left unused because Lord Vinayaka is bigger now. Many kavachams have collected there simply because Vinayaka outgrows them all!

Even today, Lord Vinayaka is inside the well and the well is always filled with water. In the monsoons, the holy waters from the well overflows and is offered to the devotees as tirtham. It is believed that Lord Ganesha forgives all the past sins of devotees who visit the temple. Visitors also resolve disputes in the temple by facing the well and vowing to speak the truth.

Source – Temple Legends

37.
MANAKULA VINAYAGAR TEMPLE AT PUDUCHERRY

This is one story that will make atheists sit back and think. It's a story about the power of the divine force. It dates back to an era when Pondicherry (now Puducherry), India, was under European rule with a European governor controlling the affairs of the town. Nepotism ruled, too, and many of the governor's friends had the liberty to interfere in any matter they deemed fit. Now one of them happened to be a hard-core atheist. Nothing wrong with that, it's a personal belief. But this man would go a step further and make fun of the faith of the natives. To the extent that he would speak ill of the idol worship in temples. The governor, as expected, gave him a free hand to do as he pleased. None dared to oppose his insensitive attitude and behaviour given the clout he held with the government.

But sooner or later karma catches up. Hand-in-glove with divine will.

One day, a temple near the sea caught his fancy. He had often seen the temple in the past and every time he went past it, he nurtured a strange desire. To throw the temple deity into the sea. That day, to entertain himself by insulting the worship rituals of that temple, he stepped inside.

Once inside, he laughed heartily at what the visitors were doing. They prostrated themselves on the ground in front of the idol. They lit incense and camphor. Broke coconuts on a slab. Some closed their eyes and muttered something. The tough tongue-twisting mantras were beyond his comprehension. And the funniest part? No doubt the idol itself. He had never seen a god like this. He had a long trunk and big ears. Bigger still was his potbelly. The most curious shape of god he had ever seen.

After his laughter subsided, he finally spoke, "What is the name given to this god?"

"Pillaiyar," answered one from his gang.

The atheist laughed harder bringing the temple to a standstill. Devotees and visitors stared at him, unable to defend neither themselves nor their Lord. Any word or action could potentially sound their death knell.

"Go and throw this stone or so-called god into the sea." He found great satisfaction in spitting out these words. He had been dying to execute this act for months now.

The thugs accompanying him swung into action. They picked up the idol and carried it out as bystanders watched helplessly. It was not an easy task and they struggled and heaved to carry Pillaiyar to the seashore. There they boarded a steamboat and went deep into the ocean to offload their baggage. The atheist watched wringing his hands in perverse joy, as they returned to tell him about the successfully accomplished mission. Inflating his chest further, he turned around to return to the temple to add salt to injury.

But what he saw there shook him up. Never had he ever experienced an episode like this! The altar which had been stripped of the idol and should have been bare, once again sported the same idol, in all its glory. Pillaiyar was standing there, even smiling maybe, as if nothing had happened. And devotees were praying to him with their head bent. Could they have brought the idol back? But how? It did not seem as though they were capable of doing anything like that.

"What happened? How did the idol return to the altar?" he asked everyone in a menacing tone, willing them to tell the truth.

"We had closed our eyes and when we opened them, Pillaiyar was back in the altar," was all they could say!

Not one to give up, the atheist once again instructed his gang of men to throw the idol into the sea. Once again, his men huffed and puffed to reach the sea carrying Pillaiyar. This time they tied him to another big rock, went into the waters and threw him hoping for success the second time around. Assured that the god was gone for good, they trudged back into the temple.

But nothing had prepared them to face Pillaiyar once again in the altar. The smiling faces of the natives increased their frustration like never before. Surely someone was messing with them, and they would teach them a lesson.

They could hear the devotees whispering, "Pillaiyar is very powerful, and no one can harm him." This was like a slap on their faces. A mere stone statue could not be stronger than them. They were ready to accept the challenge and prove who was superior. This time they would not leave anything to chance. They carried the deity back to the seashore and simultaneously the atheist emptied the temple and locked the main door. Now that everyone was out, there was no chance of anyone doing any hanky-panky. He would see how the deity returned.

He kept the key with him and accompanied the men on the boat. With his own hands he pushed the deity into the huge waves lashing at their boat. He stayed there till the stone sank into the depths of the ocean. Satisfied that this was truly the end of Pillaiyar, he went back to the temple. With an air of confidence and great drama, he unlocked the temple door. Now people would know never to antagonise him. But Pillaiyar had other ideas. He smiled back at the atheist from the altar when he entered the temple. Pillaiyar was back home, and the ball was back in the atheist's court.

"Destroy this deity with any weapon that you can find," he barked at his men, his eyes glowing with rage, "let me see if he can save himself from destruction."

He had still not given up. The men climbed into the altar and attacked the deity with sticks and crowbars. But every weapon they used was ineffective in making any impact. Not even a dent. In fact, the crowbars bounced back and shattered into pieces. Furthermore, some pieces bounced directly on the atheist striking his knee cap. He winced in pain and fell on the ground, as if prostrating himself in front of the lord. He had finally surrendered in front of a divine power.

The next morning and every morning after that, he stood in the temple silently praying to Lord Ganesha, Pillaiyar at the Manakula Vinayagar Temple at Puducherry.

Source – Temple Legends

38.
SAWAI MADHOPUR GANESHJI'S TEMPLE IN RAJASTHAN

It was the fourteenth century. Allaudin Khilji, Afghan-Turk emperor of the Khalji dynasty had assassinated his own uncle to usurp the kingdom. All that mattered to him was sitting on the throne and dominating the vast country. For that, killing even family members was not a deterrent. Once he ascended the throne, he declared himself the Sultan of Delhi and ruled with an iron hand. The subjects feared him. His wives feared him. His ministers feared him. Seeds of mutiny were planted in the soil of fear.

Allaudin Khilji had a harem of many beautiful wives and the most beautiful amongst them was Chimna. Not only was she beautiful but also passionate and ambitious. Allaudin made the mistake of ignoring her and not giving her the attention she desired. Hell hath no fury like a woman scorned. Chimna found another man who shared her passion, Muhammad Shah, a brave soldier from Allaudin's army.

Muhammad Shah, a charming man, shared a close rapport with Allaudin and had open access to his palace. Chimna thought he was right for her and proposed to him. Together they conspired to kill Allaudin. This would automatically make Muhammad king and her a queen. Lured by the trappings of wealth and power, Muhammad Shah followed Chimna's plan. However, they had underestimated Allaudin's outreach and authority. He soon discovered their game plan and Muhammad Shah, left with no option, fled for his life to avoid being killed brutally.

Although Shah saved himself from immediate assassination, his future was dark. No kingdom would give him asylum fearing Allaudin's wrath.

He had exhausted all options as far as Muslim kings were concerned. He turned to Rajput kingdoms; he had heard a lot about the valour of Rajput kings, especially Hammir Dev Chauhan. He was as fearless as a lion, and of very high character. Even in war, he followed Vedic principles of war—not attacking at night and being merciful on wounded soldiers, women, and children. His army would never stab soldiers in the back to claim quick victory. For Rajputs, killing from behind was an act of cowardice. And more than that, once they gave their word, they would sacrifice their lives for it.

A descendent of Prithviraj Chauhan, Hammir Dev Chauhan was the undisputed king of Ranthambore. Muhammad Shah knocked his door for protection. He presented himself as helpless and innocent. His compassionate plea for help moved the Rajput scion and he took him under his shelter. When Allaudin heard this, he went mad with rage. Without wasting any time, he attacked the fort of Ranthambore.

A long war waged between the two forces. Hammir Dev was weakened because some of his chief generals turned traitors and leaked out vital information. Hammir Dev locked himself and his army inside the fort. As days passed, their ration was getting exhausted. The thinning away of his supplies was extremely worrisome. Allaudin was waiting for the day when Hammir would open the fort to bring in essential supplies. As days passed, Hammir Dev's anxiety grew.

One night Lord Ganesha came in Hammir Dev's dream. Ganesha smiled benevolently at his ardent devotee. Hammir had always been devoted to Lord Ganesha. In the dream, Lord Ganesha told Hammir that all his problems were about to end. Tomorrow was a new day, Ganesha promised him.

When Hammir Dev woke up the next morning, he remembered Ganesha's promise. Soon his attendants informed him that the godowns inside the fort were brimming with food supplies. Next, he found an idol of Ganesha on one of the walls of the fort. Ganesha, sporting three eyes, had appeared himself to bless Hammir Dev.

Hammir Dev reciprocated by building a temple for Trinetra Ganesha. The third eye represents wisdom, which Ganesha is renowned for. Also accompanying him in the temple are his wives

Riddhi and Siddhi along with their sons Shubha and Labha.

This temple in Sawai Madhopur, Rajasthan receives many letters from devotees. Devotees write to Ganesha seeking his blessings before starting any new venture. The address given on the envelopes is:

Shri Ganesha Ji, Fort of Ranthambore, District – Sawai Madhopur (Rajasthan).

The postman delivers the letter with all reverence. Once delivered, the pujari reads the letter to Ganesha and keeps it at Ganesha's feet. Once Ganesha gets the invitation, all work becomes successful.

Source – Temple Legends

39.
BALLALESHWAR TEMPLE – THE ONLY TEMPLE KNOWN BY A DEVOTEE'S NAME

Little Ballal was the darling of all villagers and his friends. Pali was a sleepy village in Maharashtra where Ballal lived with his parents Kalyan and Indumati. Kalyan was the richest man in the village and his son Ballal had the best facilities possible. But little Ballal was made of a different clay. He had no interest in ordinary things other children longed for. New clothes and new toys were never on his wish list. Nor was there any kind of food that he hankered to eat. There was only one thing that he loved the most, much to his father's chagrin.

He loved to perform puja of gods, idols that he created from mud. His band of friends would join him, and this was their way of playing and having fun. The worship of mud idols which they lovingly moulded with their tiny hands. They could spend hours and hours engaged in all the steps of worshipping which Ballal had learnt by closely watching the temple *purohits.* His father could never understand why Ballal did what he did. What troubled him more was how Ballal would ever run the business that he had established. He had no other heir besides Ballal.

Oblivious to his father's concerns, everything that Ballal saw, his mind immediately thought whether it could be suitable to convert it into a temporary god and worship it. So, it was not surprising when one day he and his friends chanced upon a large stone and Ballal decided it was perfect to carry out their play of worshipping it. They had ventured out that day and reached the outskirts of the village. Since it was there that they found their object of interest, they continued to play worship on the outskirts.

Ganesha being his favourite god, Ballal decided to do Ganesha worship. His innocent and pure heart was fully engrossed in Ganesha. He performed *arti* with makeshift arti plate and incense. His friends gathered colourful flowers from nearby, which he offered to his deity. They also made mud modaks, just the way Ganesha likes them best. With great devotion, they all sat around the idol and sang songs in glorification of the devata.

While the children were busy immersed in their hearts' desires, the parents of the missing children were in agony. The children had no concept of how much time had elapsed and their parents were worried sick with every passing minute, wondering what could have happened to their children. They were nowhere to be seen. This was unlike their routine where they would be back home from wherever they were.

Just before sunset, the elders gathered to search for the missing children. They knew that Ballal usually kept them engaged with his mindless idol worship. So, they stormed into Kalyan's house demanding to know where Ballal was. In anger and anxiety, they abused Kalyan and blamed Ballal for being a freak child. Kalyan, who was already unhappy with Ballal's doings, was inflamed further.

He decided then that he would have to take stern action and stop Ballal from this madness. He instructed his servants to search for the missing children. He himself set out, heading towards the outskirts. This was a favourite place for Ballal; he loved places dotted with trees and free of humans. Many a times he had asked Kalyan to allow him to visit there. Surely, the children were there too.

And his hunch was right. As he neared Ballal's favourite spot, he could hear the high-pitched chanting of *Ganesha Ashtakam*. Again, Ballal's favourite chant. Next, he heard Ballal speaking to them quoting from the *Ganesha Purana*. If he had not been so incensed, he would have probably appreciated their dedication and Ballal's leadership qualities. But not today. Today, their musical rhythm incited more anger and a desire that he had always kept in check, suddenly exploded. Until now, he had controlled his inner voice to lash out at Ballal for not being normal. But he would not control it anymore. He would teach the boy a lesson to remember. And make him quit his peculiar way and conform to normal standards.

"Whack!"

The whacking sound jolted the children out of their trance to a gruesome sight. Ballal's father was on a breaking spree with a stick in his hand. Appearing to them like a madman brandishing a deadly weapon, he was in a destructive mood. As he stepped towards them menacingly, the frightened children ran for their lives, leaving poor Ballal behind. He had never seen his father so threatening and dangerous. He recoiled, staying a safe distance away from him. Kalyan pounced on the boy and whacked his back. Wincing in pain, Ballal let out a pitiful scream. The beating continued leaving the boy writhing with pain on the ground. Once the father had taken out all his frustration, he left the scene leaving his disowned son behind to die, tied to a tree.

In a near-unconscious state, Ballal moaned. The young boy, unfamiliar with adult complexities, had only one name on his lips. Ganesha.

"Help me Ganesha," he sent pleas to his deity, as he slipped in and out of consciousness.

Unable to ignore his young follower's calling, Ganesha appeared at the outskirts of Pali, disguised as a sadhu. Sensing divine presence, Ballal opened his eyes. Although he saw a sadhu standing in front of him, his heart recognised him as his beloved Ganesha. In the near-death condition, Ballal offered his worship to him. With one touch, Ganesha healed all of Ballal's wounds. Physical and emotional. He then spoke to Ballal.

"I am pleased with your worship of me. Ask me for any boon."

Ballal had only one desire—to continue his worship without any hindrance. So, he knew what he wanted.

"I wish that you remain here to remove the miseries for people of this village and those who take shelter in you and that I can always worship you to my heart's content."

Ganesha accepted his ardent devotee's wish and agreed to stay there. Adding his own desire, Ganesha said, "I will remain here, but your name will be put before mine so that it becomes known that I am here because of you."

One embrace, and Ganesha transformed himself into a swayambhuva deity clad in a simple dhoti kurta. As was Ganesha's desire, the temple came to be known as Ballaleshwar Temple. The stone that Ballal had worshipped and broken by his father, miraculously became whole again. It is known as Dhundi Ganesha and visitors first worship the stone before entering the temple. It is the only temple which is known by a devotee's name rather than god's name.

Source – Sthala Purana and Mudgala Purana

40.
KARUMBAYIRAM PILLAYAR TEMPLE IN TAMIL NADU

Dealings with God are so sweet, and we learn this from the Karumbayiram Pillaiyar Temple in Tamil Nadu, Kumbakonam, a temple that has been standing there for at least a thousand years, if not more. *Karumbu* in Tamil means sugarcane. Devotees offer sugarcane and garlands made from grass to Vinayaka.

This unique temple has a history dating back to Satya yuga when the demon Hiranyaksha dared to kidnap Earth to take her back with him to Pataal loka. Mother Earth, in distress, prayed for help, afraid of being ill-treated by the demon with evil intentions. Enter Lord Vishnu in His Varaha avatar to save Mother Earth. He fought the demon for thousands of years and brought Bhumi Devi back from Pataal loka. This happened in Kumbakonam and the town popularly came to be known as Varahapuri while the temple came to be known as Varahapuri Vinayaka temple.

A thousand years ago, something miraculous happened and the deity was renamed as Karumbayiram Pillaiyar – Varaha.

There lived a sugarcane trader in a village near this sleepy temple town. He conducted his business shrewdly and in a very miserly manner to make maximum profits. Without hiring any help, he carted sugarcane from his field to the sugarcane crushing mills on a weekly basis. By divine intervention, his route took him through Varahapuri Vinayaka temple.

One seemingly ordinary day, his throat felt parched as he passed the temple. He stopped at the temple tank to refresh himself. The sparkling water gave him vigour to continue on his journey with renewed energy. Just as he sat on the cart, a plump short boy appeared in his path, blocking his movement. Irritated at the nuisance created by the boy, he asked him, "Boy, why have you blocked my way? Move aside."

The boy cheekily asked the trader to give him a piece of sugarcane from his cart.

"I only want the sweet sugarcane. Please give me a piece."

Naturally, the trader had no intention of parting with even a single piece of sugarcane and incur a loss. He calculated that if the boy stopped him every week then in a year, he would be facing a whopping loss. Shaking his head he said, "No, no, move aside." His mind had immediately magnified the small act of kindness to an annual business loss.

By then, some people had gathered to see what was going on and why the boy had blocked the trader. Many felt sorry for the boy. He was only asking for a piece of sugarcane. Nothing really valuable as such. They requested the trader to hand over a small piece, but the trader refused.

In order to convince the trader that giving was good karma, someone even pointed out how the boy had a potbelly, just like Varahapuri Vinayaka. Considering the mounting pressure on him, the trader accelerated his thought process. He had to get out of this sticky situation somehow before he was forced to lighten his cart for the insignificant boy standing in front of him. What was more, the boy had the audacity to be grinning too. That bothered him even more, as if he delighted in looting him.

Miffed by the entire scene, he said the first thing that came to his mind. "This is not sweet sugarcane but only salty sticks. They become sweet only after crushing them. I'm sorry but you will not want to eat dry salty stick, would you?"

The boy hung his head in disappointment. They sure looked like juicy sugarcane to him. His supporters too dispersed on hearing the man's excuse. There was nothing more to say. The boy then, in a flash of anger, said, "It's okay if they are really salty sticks!" and he gave the trader a hard look which somehow made him jittery. The boy then vanished into thin air. *What did the boy mean by that? And where did he disappear? Like a ghost!* He wondered about this throughout the journey, unable to come to any conclusion about the significance of the boy or the statement.

He soon reached the crushing mill and offloaded his cart. Happy to have accomplished his work for the day, and dismissing the boy from his mind, he was about to turn back when the mill staff called out to him.

"What have you delivered today?" they asked crossly.

The trader stared at them. "Sugarcane," he said.

"This is not sugarcane but grass sticks. Are you trying to swindle us?"

Alarmed at the accusation, the trader's thoughts instantly went back to the boy's weird look and comment. *Was it a paranormal experience? Was the boy a ghost? A troublemaker ghost?*

He apologised to the mill staff and with a heavy heart he collected all his sugarcane turned grass sticks again. By the time he reached home, his heart was as dark as the moonless evening sky. He wanted to forget the disheartening events of the day and sleep quickly. That night, Varahapuri Vinayaka visited him in a dream. Surprisingly, the lord chastised him for lying to him. "All I had asked for was a piece of sugarcane. But you lied. You have been rewarded for your lies."

The trader got up with a jerk. Vinayaka . . . sugarcane . . . the boy . . . his head was muddled with all these thoughts. He slowly got clarity on awaking fully realising that Lord Vinayaka had punished him for lying. Remorseful and repentant at his petty lying, he rushed to the temple as soon as dawn broke, taking his cart with him. He fell at the feet of Lord Vinayaka and asked for forgiveness. Of course, the lord was kind-hearted and merciful enough to forgive the trader. He also transformed the grass sticks back into sugarcane. The jubilant man rushed into the temple to offer a bundle of sugarcanes to the Lord.

Since that day, the Varahapuri Vinayaka became Karumbayiram Vinayaka. (In Tamil, *Karumbu* means sugarcane and *aayiram* means thousand.) Following the trend, devotees flock to the temple to offer as many sugarcane sticks to their beloved Karumbayiram Vinayaka. Another understanding is that a thousand of grass sticks in the cart became sugarcane sticks. Hence the number thousand.

Source – Temple Legends

41.
MILAGU PILLAIYAR TEMPLE IN TAMIL NADU

This Ganesha temple has a unique *abhisheka* process. When rainfall is scanty, devotees first grind pepper on the Ganesha idol and then perform abhisheka with water. The peppered water flows into an adjoining canal and this guarantees a healthy rainfall. Milagu Pillaiyar Temple in Tamil Nadu, dating back to twenty centuries, has a history behind this unique ritual.

A king in Kerala was facing a difficult situation. He had an incurable disease. His doctors had tried every possible remedy in the book, but none helped. Days passed and his condition deteriorated. Mentally, he was preparing himself to leave the world. But then, a miracle happened.

One night, he was tossing in bed, overwhelmed by pain, when he heard a celestial sound. The sound was definitely not coming from any earthly source. In fact, he couldn't find the source. It seemed to be echoing from above. He was confused. Was he awake or was he dreaming? Anyway, that was not important. What was important was the message. He heard the voice giving him an instruction.

"Build a doll as tall as you. Fill it up with pearls and emeralds, the size of pulses. Transfer your disease to the doll. Then donate the doll to a brahman. Once the doll is donated in charity, the disease will leave you."

Overjoyed, the king immediately gave orders to build a doll of his stature. He got it filled with jewels exactly as instructed. That was the easy part. The difficult part was finding a brahman. Normally that is not the difficult part. But in his case, it was. For, who would be willing to accept disease in charity? No one, naturally. Not one brahman in the kingdom was willing to oblige the king.

However, the lure of precious jewels prompted a brahman from Karnataka to accept the offer. When he heard about the king's dilemma, he empathised with him. He thought it would be a good idea to help him and accept the wealth which he could use for welfare purposes. As far as contracting the disease was concerned, he felt it was a matter of destiny. There was nothing in his control as far as disease and death were concerned. He presented himself to the king and humbly accepted the charity.

As soon as the doll transferred hands, it came alive. It demanded from the young lad that he offer part of the benefits of his meditation and spiritual practices as penalty to keep himself free of disease. The brahman had no option but to relent and give in to the doll. However, he wanted to use the wealth for a good cause. He considered many ways he could help people, but none seemed right. Feeding the poor, building a school, building a temple, helping other brahmans . . . he considered and rejected all of them. He wanted to do something that would have a far greater impact than all of these put together.

When in doubt, ask someone wise. Going by this maxim, he decided to take Sage Agastya's counsel.

The only problem was it would take him a few days to reach him. Fearing the safety of his treasure, he handed over the doll to a trustworthy friend, asking him to keep it in his custody till he returned.

Sage Agastya, through his psychic abilities, knew that this boy was coming to meet him for advice. He wanted to test his sincerity. Was he truly determined to commit to a welfare project? Or was it just a show-off mission? He would know soon. The sage planted many obstacles on the brahman's path. The boy went through sudden and intense weather changes, sometimes freezing, sometimes sweating. He went for days without food and water. He travelled over thorny and rocky paths ignoring the blisters and wounds on his feet. But he never gave up. He finally made it to the sage's ashram.

The sage was mighty pleased. It was truly a deep desire to do good. Even though he knew it, he asked the boy to tell him his problem. The traveller revealed his story of how he had accepted wealth in charity from the king of Kerala at great risk so that he could use that money for the benefit of society at large.

"I desperately need a cause that will help the maximum people in the long term."

Sage Agastya, who had already been instrumental in forming the Kaveri River, suggested that he create a water body.

"Water is the most precious thing that sustains life. When villages face drought, they lose life and cattle. How helpful it would be to have a canal that took care of all water needs.

"On your way back, you will meet a cow. Follow the cow noting the route and dig a canal along that route. Build dams where she leaves dung and storage tanks where she urinates. The place she rests will be the location for lake. The place where she disappears will be the end of the canal."

Amazed at the instructions, the brahman boy nodded his head. It was the most fantastic experience of his life. Tracing the route taken by the cow, he finally reached his village. To get his doll and wealth back, he met his friend. Unknown to him, his friend had removed the precious gems from his doll. Only after reaching home did he realise that his own friend had swindled him. How would he execute his water project without his resources? He had no option but to approach the king and ask for his intervention.

The king called the friend and asked him to speak the truth in front of the deity of Lord Shiva. The friend still swore in front of the deity, denying any theft. As a result of blatant lying and sinning, the friend burst into instant flames.

The brahman was finally able to complete his dream. He did exactly as per the advice of Sage Agastya, digging canals, building dams, and storage tanks. The cow disappeared at Prancheri, where a huge lake stands even today. It is a vast expanse of water, as huge as a sea.

Great souls never hanker for publicity. Nor did the brahman youth from Karnataka. No one knows his name. The canal was thus named after his mother tongue, Kannada. He installed a Vinayaka temple at the Kannadian Kalvai canal. Abhisheka of the deity flowed into the canal and that was the signal for heavens to pour rain. He established the pepper abhisheka, a ritual hitherto unknown in any other temple. When the pepper water flows into the canal, it is time for the monsoon clouds to rush in and do their job.

Source – Puranic Legends

42.
VIGHNESHWAR TEMPLE IN MAHARASHTRA

Satya yuga, one of the four yugas in the Vedic time cycle, was known for elaborate and opulent fire sacrifices. Yet again, a cloud of smoke from a sacrificial arena was seen in the skyline while the fragrance of offerings wafted in the air, indicating a sacrifice in progress. Pious kings continually performed Vedic sacrifices for the welfare of their subjects.

One such king was King Abhinandan, the ruler of Hemavatim. He had performed such a large number of sacrifices that Indra felt his throne was shaking. What if King Abhinandan managed to replace him as the king of heaven? The mere thought made him jittery. He wrung his hands so violently that they nearly fell off.

Till now, Indra had watched as a mute spectator as Abhinandan performed sacrifice after sacrifice. But no longer could he afford the luxury of remaining a spectator. He had to do something at once to put an end to it. In fact, he had to put an end to this very sacrifice lest it ended his reign in heaven. Without wasting a moment, he approached Kaala. Only Kaala could do what he had in mind.

Kaala agreed to Indra's proposal to disrupt the sacrifice. Not just this but any other sacrifice thereafter. Not just Abhinandan but anyone who performed sacrifices would face so many obstacles that they would be forced to abandon it. There could be many more kings like Abhinandan eyeing his throne.

And who could fight with Kaala? His intervention effectively ended all sacrifices. The number of sacrifices dwindled day by day. Till the skyline became a clear blue with no smoke anywhere. So successful was he that he earned the title of Vighnasura. A demon who is an obstacle. A demon who creates difficulties. A day came when all Vedic rites and rituals along with dharma disappeared from earth.

This created immense problems for the devatas. They looked forward to accepting offerings from the sacrifices and with that having ended, there were absolutely no oblations. They got together and meditated on Gajanana to come and relieve them of the consequences. Ganesha is always in active mode to go anywhere he is called. Hearing the woes of devatas, his heart melted, and he decided to take the battle to Vighnasura on earth.

Taking birth as the son of a sage, he swiftly descended on earth to resolve the issue. Lord Shiva then approached the sage seeking permission for Ganesha to fight the demon. Naturally, the sage was frightened but Ganesha convinced him that he was capable enough to deal with any adversity. Equipping himself with his *ankush* (hook), he went in search of the demon. Vighnasura was an expert in the art of creating illusions. He dodged Ganesha's ankush by constantly shifting forms. From cyclone to flood to fire, he changed shapes continually in a bid to force Ganesha into submission. Ganesha combatted all the shapes destroying all the illusions. Neither cyclone nor flood nor fire could make any impact.

Vighnasura finally realised that his strength was no match for his powerful opponent, and it would be wiser to surrender. He fell at Ganesha's feet begging for shelter. Ganesha extracted a promise from him. In future, he would not harass his devotees. Nor would he come in their way. If a person became forgetful of Ganesha before starting anything new, only then could Vighnasura put obstacles in the way. Vighnasura accepted all his conditions and humbly asked Ganesha to be known as Vighneshwar, the remover of all obstacles.

Vighneshwar Temple is one of the Ashtavinayak temples in Ozar, Maharashtra.

Source – Mudgala Purana

SECTION 3:

Ganesha Prayers

VAKRATUNDA GANESHA MANTRA

Dedicated to Lord Ganesha, Goddess Riddhi (Goddess of prosperity) and Goddess Siddhi (Goddess of spiritual enlightenment). This mantra helps invoke Lord Ganesha's blessings of wealth, prosperity, wisdom, success, and good fortune without any obstacles in life.

Vakratunda Maha-Kaaya Surya-Koti Samaprabha
Nirvighnam Kuru Me Deva Sarva-Kaaryeshu
Sarvadaa ||

With a curved trunk, a huge and powerful body, and dazzling aura of crores of suns, O' God, please remove all obstacles from my life forever.

GANESHA GAYATRI MANTRA

Modesty, righteousness, and wisdom are the benefits of chanting this mantra. Guru Parshuram, in a duel, threw an axe at Lord Gajanan, which was a gift to him by his father. In order to honour his father, Ganesha showed humility and modesty by not fighting back. Thus, he lost one tusk. One tusk implies singular unbranched concentration in meditation.

Aum Ekadantaya Vidmahe, Vakratundaya Dhimahi, Tanno Danti Prachodayat ||

We meditate upon the single-tusked Elephant God who is omnipresent. We pray for greater intellect to the curved trunk Lord. By bowing before the single-tusked elephant Lord, may we get illuminated with wisdom.

BASIC GANAPATI MANTRA

Chant this mantra to ward off negativities from one's life; to ensure success in all new ventures.

Om Gam Ganpataye Namah II

Bow down to Lord Ganapati in all faith and accept his great qualities to pervade our being.

SHRI SANKAT NASHANAM GANESHA STOTRAM

The *Ganesha stotram* is in *Narada Purana*. It is all-auspicious because it destroys all impediments and sorrows forever. *Sankat* means troubles and *nashanam* means to destroy forever. So, by chanting this prayer, one can remove problems forever. Narada says that Ganesha's various names should be called out three times a day to remove all fears.

Pranamya shirasa devam Gauri putram Vinayakam.
Bhakthavasam smaretrityamayuh kama
artha sidhaye ||1||

Salute with your head to Lord Ganapati, the son of Goddess Parvati, if you are learned and wish for more life, wealth, and love.

Prathamam Vakratundam cha,
Ekadantam dwitiyakam.
Tritiyam Krushna Pingaksham,
Gajavaktram Chaturthakam ||2||

Remember him as the god with broken tusk first, as the Lord with one tusk second, as the one with reddish black eyes third, and one who has the face of an elephant fourth.

Lambodaram Panchamam cha,
Sashtam Vikatamev cha.
Saptamam Vighnarajam cha,
Dhoomravarnam tathashtamam ||3||

Remember him as the one who has a very broad paunch fifth, sixth as the one who is cruel to his enemies. As the one who is remover of obstacles seventh, and eighth as the one who is of the colour of smoke.

Navamam Bhalchandram cha,
Dashamam tu Vinayakam.
Ekadasham Ganapatim,
Dwadasham tu Gajananam ||4||

Ninth as the one with crescent on his forehead, as the leader of remover of obstacles tenth. Eleventh as the leader of the army of Lord Shiva, and twelfth as the one with the face of an elephant.

Dwadasaithani namani,
Trisandhyam yah pathenara.
Na cha vighna bhayam tasya,
Sarvsiddhi karam param ||5||

By reading these twelve names at dawn, noon, and dusk, one can get rid of the fear of defeat and achieve whatever he wants.

Vidhyarthi labhate Vidhyam,
Danarthi labhate Dhanam.
Putrarthi labhate Putran,
Moksharthi labhate Gateem ||6||

Students who pursue education will get knowledge. Those who seek wealth will get wealth. Those wishing for a son, will get a son and those wanting salvation will get salvation.

Japet Ganapati stotram,
Shadbhirmasai phalam labheth.
Samvatsarena sidhim cha,
Labhate natra sanshaya ||7||

By chanting this prayer to Ganapati, visible results are seen within six months.

And within a year, all wishes are fulfilled. There is no doubt about this.

Ashtabhyo Brahmoyashr Likihitwa yh samarpayet.
Tasya Vidhya bhavetsarva Ganeshasya
Prasadatah ||8||

One who shares this prayer in writing with eight wise people, gets blessings of Ganesha. Ganesha bestows knowledge and all good qualities on him.

|| Iti Shri Narad Purane Sankat nashanam Ganesha
Stotram Sampurnam ||

Thus ends the prayer from *Narada Purana* to Ganesha, which can destroy all sorrows.

BRAHMA - SAMHITA (5.50)

This prayer is taken from the fifth chapter of the hymns of *Brahma-Samhita*.

yat-pāda-pallava-yugaṁ vinidhāya kumbha-
dvandve praṇāma-samaye sa gaṇādhirājaḥ
vighnān vihantum alam asya jagat-trayasya
govindam ādi-puruṣaṁ tam ahaṁ bhajāmi

I worship Govinda, the primeval Lord, whose lotus feet are always held by Gaṇesha. Thus, by offering obeisance with the help of *tumuli* protruding from his elephant head, Ganesha obtains his powers of destroying all obstacles that arise on the path of progress in any of the three worlds.

About the Author

Shubha Vilas is a lifestyle coach, storyteller and author. He studied patent law after completing his engineering degree but finally chose the path of a spiritual seeker.

Ramayana: The Game of Life is his bestselling series. He's also the author of *Open-Eyed Meditations, Mystical Tales for a Magical Life* and *Perfect Love: 5.5 Ways to a Lasting Relationship*. The focus of his work is the application of scriptural wisdom to day-to-day life and addressing the needs of corporates and the youth through thought-provoking seminars.

He has delivered more than 5000 talks, inspiring more than 5,25,000 people, across twenty countries in the last ten years. He is a visiting faculty at several premier business management schools in India including the Indian Institute of Management (IIM) and Narsee Monjee Institute of Management Studies (NMIMS), Mumbai.

He has also been a guest speaker at the prestigious Massachusetts Institute of Technology (MIT), Boston; Dresden International University, Germany; WITS, Johannesburg and several centres of Indian Institute of Technology in India. He is on the advisory board of MIT Pune's online education system.

He has also spoken at Google, Microsoft, Amazon, Samsung at their world headquarters at USA.

To know more about him, visit www.shubhavilas.com.